You Can't Be Mexican

Frank S. Mendez

You Can't Be Mexican

You Talk Just Like Me

Frank S. Mendez

The Kent State University Press

KENT & LONDON

© 2005 by The Kent State University Press, Kent, Ohio 44242

ALL RIGHTS RESERVED

Library of Congress Catalog Card Number 2004019208

ISBN 0-87338-822-4

Manufactured in the United States of America

08 07 06 05 04   5 4 3 2 1

LIBRARY OF CONGRESS CATALOGING-IN-PUBLICATION DATA

Mendez, Frank S., 1925–

You can't be Mexican, you talk just like me / Frank S. Mendez.

p.   cm.—(Voices of Diversity)

ISBN 0-87338-822-4 (hardcover : alk. paper) ∞

1. Mendez, Frank S., 1925–

2. Mexican Americans—Ohio—Lorain—Biography.

3. Immigrants—Ohio—Lorain—Biography.

4. Lorain (Ohio)—Biography.

5. Lorain (Ohio)—Ethnic relations.

6. Michoacán de Ocampo (Mexico)—Biography.

I. Title.   II. Series

F499.L8M46 2005

305.8968'72077123—dc22   2004019208

British Library Cataloging-in-Publication data are available.

To the Memory of
María Tovar
and
Josefa Guardia de Lombardo

Contents

Foreword

JOHN J. GRABOWSKI, SERIES EDITOR

The story of immigration to and migration within America is one in which history and heritage are in constant competition. Because the recounting of coming "here" from some other place is so central to many of our lives or family histories, that saga becomes part of our heritage. Heritage, as David Lowenthal argues in his book *The Heritage Crusade and the Spoils of History,* is different from history in that it represents more of what we want to believe about ourselves than what actually happened.

The dynamic tension between heritage and history forms the foundation of Voices of Diversity, a new series of publications by the Kent State University Press. Voices of Diversity will republish, in English translation, existing memoirs and accounts of immigrant and migrant life in northeastern Ohio. It will also publish new first-person works relating to this topic. Frank Mendez's autobiographical account, *You Can't Be Mexican: You Talk Just Like Me,* is the first volume in this series.

Like any other memoir, this volume might, at initial glance, be considered an exercise in heritage rather than history, as it recounts what the author chooses to or is able to recall. Yet within the field of immigration history, the best autobiographies can serve as an antidote to the general aura of heritage that now tinges the American immigrant story. Personal accounts often provide a reality check to the pleasant generalities that tend to form the image of what we wish to believe about immigrants. They can challenge our concepts about family solidarity and the immigrant work ethic, and revise our image of the "good old immigrant neighborhood."

You Can't Be Mexican does provide alternative views of such facets of immigrant life, but it also serves as what one might call a corrective to broader issues. Most importantly, it prompts us to think more carefully about our vision of the "ethnic heritage" of the industrial Midwest. There is a tendency to believe that the human fuel for the incredible industrial expansion around the Great Lakes in the late nineteenth and early twentieth century came from Europe, particularly from eastern and southern Europe. Indeed, the Paul Bunyan of the steel mills was named Joe Magarac—a brawny fictional character from central Europe. One could argue that the ascription of a European immigrant character to the mills and factories of mid-America became stronger as the industrial era of the Great Lakes waned. Today, three generations distant from the great European immigration at the turn of the century, the descendants of those immigrants tend to celebrate their families' contribution to industrial America. It is a mark of pride, in some ways every bit as potent as the pioneer heritage claimed by earlier generations of Americans. The opening of the museum at Ellis Island (the main gateway for the great European immigration) in 1990 signified the national acceptance of and pride in the European industrial migration to the United States. One could argue that today Ellis Island assumes the same mythical importance for these Americans as Plymouth Rock did one hundred years earlier for those who came from different European shores.

Certainly, the bulk of the labor in industrial mid-America was European or African in origin. However, Frank Mendez reminds us that the history of the region is more diverse. Mendez tells us that industrial communities such as Lorain were more polyglot than we tend to remember. He also tells us other things that somehow get lost in the way we view immigrant heritage. Yes, his parents worked the fields. That fits the image we have of Mexican immigrants. But they also came to the mills and factories of the Midwest. Many contemporary Americans find this surprising—just as surprising as the fact that Chicago had one of the largest Mexican populations in North America in the 1920s. Mexican immigrants picked crops, but they also made steel in Lorain and Gary and Chicago and built automobiles in Detroit. Certainly the surge in Chicano and Latino historical studies in the past three decades has filled out this story in the corridors of academe, but in the corridors of Midwestern heritage it is not a widely recognized story. For many Americans, Mexicans are "new" immigrants confined in large part to the service industries of America. They are not totally so now, nor were they in the past that is described in this memoir.

Frank Mendez opens his memoir with a powerful family tale about the manner in which his father escaped the violence of the great Mexican Revolution. Here again relating a personal heritage serves as a means to illuminate history and to bring a fresh perspective with which to view generalizations about immigration. Natividad Mendez fled one of the largest and most violent revolutions in the Americas in the twentieth century—a decade-long revolt that cost tens of thousands of lives and forever changed the nation of Mexico. It was not unlike the revolts, famines, wars, and persecutions that set many Europeans in motion—events that are forever fixed in the popular and scholarly story of that phenomenon. In an era when some are tempted to see Mexicans solely as economic migrants, Frank Mendez causes us to reexamine a popular image and, perhaps, to become more curious about a nearby but largely unknown aspect of a shared continental history.

In these and other ways, *You Can't Be Mexican* opens new perspectives on the immigrant history of northeastern Ohio and challenges readers to think again about how we choose to characterize a region, a period of time, and a group of people. That is one of its values. However, its chief value remains in the fact that it is a memoir in which the story of one family, and one individual, Frank Mendez, is played out against a backdrop of local, national, and international events. As individuals interested, likely as not, in our own histories and heritages, we identify with the story he relates and become involved and concerned with some of the key issues of the immigrant. As Frank Mendez moves from field to town, from school to the military, and then to a career, we, like he, are prompted to look closely at how we have decided to see ourselves in a region, nation, and world layered with diverse identities and to ask how our heritage fits into that region's history.

Acknowledgments

The expression of the many thanks that I owe to those who have participated meaningfully in the publication of this book must begin with members of my family. Chief among them is Leticia Carles Guardia Mendez, my wife of more than fifty years, who, as always, was there for me when I needed her. She enabled me to concentrate on this work by assuming much of my share of our family responsibilities. In fact, she has initiated similar arrangements throughout our marriage, while always meeting the demands of her two successful careers, first, as a brilliant head of household of a family of five children and an oftentimes distracted husband and father who too frequently confounded his obligations to family and profession, and second as a successful teacher whose career did not end with her retirement from the Department of Defense Dependents Schools System—she instilled in our children the same principles that she instilled in her students (our nuclear family holds eleven college degrees, six of them earned by our three daughters).

Carol Alvarado, Terry Scarlata, and Jo Mendez, my daughters, were my "worst" critics. They identified the occasional conflict between statements in different sections of the manuscript, suggested improvements and confirmed the validity of sentences crafted from my research efforts. Their persistent demands for a first-class product came across to me as "payback time" for their having to adhere to the standards my wife and I required of them in their early years.

My beloved sisters, Mary Palmer, Josie Espinoza, and Jessie Arizmendi, sent me documents, photos, and notes that resurrected my childhood memories. Mary coordinated submissions from others in our extended family. She provided insight, described possible productive leads, and conducted research to develop key facts. It is quite possible that without her continuing encouragement and support this book would not have been written. José Jesus Mendez, my half-brother, forwarded important documents and other information concerning our father. My first cousin, Dolores Aguilar Gonzalez, filled a void in my story by contributing anecdotes pertaining to the family life of her parents; her mother and mine were very close until my mother's untimely death. My late Aunt Andrea, widow of my Uncle Manuel Silva, well into her eighties at the time, described for me with a clear mind her family's crossing of the Rio Grande at Eagle Pass to work the cotton and sugar beet fields of Big Spring, Texas.

Margaret Scott had the audacity to consider me a promising author after reviewing a very rough draft that my daughter, Carol, let her read. Margaret's encouraging words and excellent suggestions were delivered at just the right moment; her review was the first by an outside-the-family reader.

A special thanks is due Dr. John J. Grabowski, series editor of Voices of Diversity. We met two years ago through a casual telephone call I made to the Western Reserve Historical Society in Cleveland, Ohio, where he was serving as acting library director. I inquired about his organization's interest in the unpublished genealogical account I had written about the extended families of my grandparents. He acknowledged that a document concerning Mexican American life in Northeastern Ohio was of historic interest to the Society. So began a personal association that, with his guidance and support, resulted in the Kent State University Press editorial board approving the publication of *You Can't Be Mexican*.

I am indebted to Joanna Hildebrand Craig, acquiring editor of the Kent State University Press, for believing in me throughout what seemed to be a long review process. Now that she has helped to make me a published author, I realize that a lengthy processing time is necessary in the publishing business.

I am grateful for Raymond J. Heine's gracious loan of the sole remaining copy of his late wife's out-of-print *Come Reminisce with Me: A History of Glidden, Texas, 1885–1985*. Dorothy Jean Heine's vivid presentation of the lives of several Mexican and Mexican American families in Glidden in the early 1920s reinforced my understanding of the Mendez family's experience in that town.

I have to thank three couples for helping me to appreciate the Panama years: Doctors Carlos Ivan Zuniga Guardia and Sidia Candanedo de Zuniga; Engineer Luis Archuleta and Olda Calres de Archuleta; and Engineer Nestor Jaramillo and Gloria de Jaramillo indulged me with hundreds of conversations about Panama, its history, and its people. My six friends are highly regarded in their respective fields and have impressive accomplishments.

Carlos Ivan Zuniga Guardia is former rector of the 75,000-student University of Panama and is currently a columnist for *La Prensa,* the most widely read newspaper in Panama. The president of Panama named him in 2003 as the Abanderado del Centenario, with the honor of bearing the Panama flag in a march over the Panama City streets in celebration of the one-hundredth anniversary of the founding of the Republic of Panama. Doctor Zuniga received his Doctorado en Derecho Publico from the Universidad Nacional de San Marcos in Lima, Peru—the oldest university in the Americas—and he was elected as a deputy of the unicameral Asamblea de Panama.

Sydia Candanedo de Zuniga is a famous poetess in Panama and Latin America. She has published over half a dozen books of poetry, essays, and anthologies and has been awarded the Premio Miro (Poesia, 1969) and (Cuento, 1999). The Premio Miro is the Panama equivalent of the Pulitzer Prize. She received the Doctorado en Educacion, majoring in Castellano and Literatura from the Universidad Nacional de San Marcos and is a retired professor from the University of Panama.

Luis Archuleta is the retired chief of the engineering division of the Panama Canal Company. The Archuletas own and operate the Santa Fe Cattle Ranch; they are recognized as outstanding leaders of the Panama interior.

Nestor Jaramillo is a retired engineer with a successful career working for various commercial and industrial firms. Gloria de Jaramillo retired as a teacher in the Canal Zone Schools system; she currently dedicates her life to working as a volunteer in many projects of the Catholic Church.

While I have correctly identified relatives and close friends in *You Can't Be Mexican,* I have changed the names of other persons to protect their right to privacy. In some cases I have used composites of conversations, although the essential meaning remains intact. Finally, I regret not being able to identify the many others who may have contributed to this book—a comment, a word, a look—and apologize for any possible misinterpretation of their interactions with me. Any errors in this book are solely my responsibility.

❀ ❀ ❀

CHAPTER ONE

Michoacán, Mexico

It was September 1946, and I had recently completed a tour of active duty in the United States Marine Corps. Before starting college classes, I accompanied my father on a trip from my hometown in Ohio to his birthplace in Michoacán, Mexico.

We were met at the Los Reyes train station by a cousin who led us on horseback over the mountain trail to the village of Zirosto. After several days of meeting and mixing with members of the extended family, we gathered one evening in the "living area" of the simple tin-roofed house in which my father had been born. My uncle, Tío Marcos, held the group spellbound by recounting details of the departure of his brother, Natividad, or Nati, for the United States thirty years earlier.

"Nati, *ayúdame*," he said. "Help me out with details that I am not aware of or do not remember."

Together they carried the story of my father's emigration from Mexico to Texas.

❀

"Nati, Nati, *Despierta!* Wake up! The *Zapatistas* are coming! Go, Go!" His sister shouted. "They know you are with the government, and they have shot a soldier in one of the upper villages."

The undisguised fear in her voice did not need to be accompanied by her terror-driven words or her agitated shaking of Natividad's spindly bunk. The civil defense militiaman knew at once that he was in danger of being shot by Emiliano Zapata's approaching *guerrilleros*. Panic-stricken, he launched himself from the scrap-cloth quilt mattress, and dashed barefooted across the hard-packed dirt floor of the adobe hut toward the Z-braced wood-slat rear door where his mother stood. She was crying, quietly playing her rehearsed role, leaning tremulously against the open door, holding out his worn leather *huaraches,* handwoven cotton trousers, and long-sleeved blouse.

"*Coje!* Take them, *mi amor,*" she sobbed.

He snatched his clothes out of her hands, dodged her ad-libbed attempted embrace, and shot into the moonlit night of a Mexican mountain village of the early twentieth century.

He barely heard the last words she was ever to address to him: "*Vaya con Dios, mi'jo. Te quiero.*"

Racing along the beaten footpath leading to the steep declivity that formed the rear boundary of the lot, he created a modern dance movement—hop, hop, one foot into a *huarache*; hop, hop, the other foot into the other *huarache*; hop, hop, one leg into a trouser leg; hop, hop, his other leg into the other trouser leg; stride, stride, an arm into a blouse sleeve; stride, stride, the other arm into the other sleeve; stride, stride, his head into the blouse opening. Bang! Bang! The movement ended as bullets whizzed by him, and he tripped over the lot's edge, tumbling downward, arms and legs flailing, unable to arrest his fall by digging his fingers into the toeholds he had carved into the dry arroyo's sloping bank.

He cried out, "*Ay, Mamá. Adiós, Mamacita. Te quiero!*"

In that split second, fear had yielded to guilt. His state of absolution ended as his body slammed into the pebble-strewn dirt bed of the arroyo. The dazed twenty-year-old picked himself up, and took some tentative steps. Discovering no apparent broken bones, Natividad started running, bouncing off the passageway's winding walls, motivated by gunshots and bullets striking the arroyo's bed and walls behind him.

The shooting stopped on a *guerrillero's* shout: "*Mierda! Se escapó.* Shit! He got away. We'll never find him. We don't know the territory."

His spirits lifting, Natividad continued his narrow escape through familiar territory, working his way out of the arroyo several miles in the downstream direction. At daybreak he felt confident that the *guerrilleros* would not spend much time and effort searching for an insignificant militiaman of the lowest rank, one who had been forced into the local militia in compliance with the government's policy of drafting young men in every village under its jurisdiction into local defense units. They received little training and were forced to acquire their own weapons, often obsolete rifles and pistols more dangerous to the shooter than to the intended target. He knew he could not return to his home in Zirosto as long as the revolutionaries controlled that part of the State of Michoacán.

As Uncle Marcos continued the story, I silently vowed to do research on the State of Michoacán and the Mexican migrant experience (an intention that, like those of more than a few twenty-year-olds, was delayed for several decades).

Much of Michoacán lies in the *altiplanicie,* the high-altitude intermountain plateau bounded by the Sierra Madre Occidental mountain range on the west, the Sierra Madre del Sur chain on the south, the Sierra Madre Oriental range (a prolongation of the American Rockies separated by the Rio Grande Valley) on the east, and the Anáhuac Cordillera running between the western and eastern Sierra Madres. Zirosto is located in the Anáhuac Cordillera, a range consisting of numerous active volcanoes (including the well-known Popocatépetl and the younger Paricutín, which came into existence in 1943 when molten lava began to ooze from a fissure in a cornfield near Paricutín, a neighboring village of Zirosto).

At this point, my father took over the story.

As the sun peeked over the nearby mountaintop, spreading its warm brightness, he climbed a large boulder to get a better view of what lay ahead and looked toward Los Reyes, the closest town with rail and bus connections to *El Norte.* It lay more than a hard day's walk on the horse trail connecting the town with the higher mountain villages. He had walked down that path before, accompanied by other Zirosto men on their northward journey to and across the *Rio Bravo del Norte,* seeking stoop labor jobs in the *betabel,* the sugar beet fields of the American Midwest.

He reviewed his situation. *"No puedo regresar a mi casa.* I cannot return to Zirosto, and I have no relatives or close friends outside the village with whom I can wait out the revolution. I have to consider the hazardous trip to Texas with no money and no companions to join for an increased measure of protection. I am aware of what awaits me if I choose to travel to the United States."

He had returned from his previous trip to the United States after the *betabel* growing season, with more *pesos* (in dollars) than he could have earned in one year at a full-time job in Mexico. But he had no desire to return to the *betabel* next season, or ever again. If he were to return to the United States it would be to seek other work. He started out for Los Reyes, not sure that he had made the right decision.

The trail ran along a ridgeline formed by an ancient lava flow, flattened by eons of exposure to erosive elements and now overgrown by sparse vegetation. From time to time he scurried off the trail into the underbrush or hid behind the hump of a raised shoulder whenever he heard approaching horses or the faint sound of voices in the distance.

Crouching low, he thought, "*Caramba*, they're still looking for me."

He calmed down after confirming that it was not the *guerrilleros* on the trail. As the sun rose higher toward noon and the countryside assumed corresponding elevated temperatures, he rested at a gurgling artesian spring to drink the refreshing water and reflect on the coming trip to *El Estado de Tejas*. He would have to walk long distances, sometimes hopping a ride by clinging to the top cargo rail of a lumbering, overcrowded bus, his toes supporting his weight by resting on the lower side molding of the rickety transport vehicle. Other times he would trot alongside a train leaving the station, awaiting the instant when the conductor's helpers were momentarily distracted by trying to prevent other ticketless men from climbing aboard. He remembered how he jumped on the lower step, simultaneously grabbed the vertical handlebar, and squeezed past the guards, disappearing into the packed interior.

He arose from the stream bank and continued the long walk to Los Reyes. At the town's edge he stopped at a farmhouse and approached a man standing at the gate.

"*Buenos días*," said Nati. "I'm not a *Zapatista*. I'm on my way to *los Estados Unidos*, and I have not eaten since yesterday. Can you spare me a little food and some old clothes?"

"*Buenos días*," said the farmer. "You don't look like a *Zapatista*. We can offer you a taco and an old shirt. We have nothing more to give. We are very poor."

At another house, he received a taco of refried beans, some well-worn clothes, and an old straw sombrero, distorted from its original shape by the sun and rain. He had observed those same humane gestures in Zirosto—the unhesitant sharing by poor Mexican families of their meager resources with the less fortunate. He was confident that these kind acts by impoverished *peons* would be duplicated several times on the way to the Rio Grande.

Undaunted, Natividad headed for the Los Reyes train station.

❀

Uncle Marcos picked up the lead from my father and continued the story. "In Zirosto, our parents, José María Mendez and María Librada Ynojosa, and the four other children were relieved that Natividad was still alive, but we were not sure if he would ever return."

The family knew that life in Zirosto for a young man, as in most Mexican villages of the times, did not offer any real opportunities for him to rise above the socioeconomic level to which he was born. One tended to remain throughout his lifetime in that same class. The evening of his departure was the last time my father's parents were ever to see their oldest child.

I learned that there had been only a handful of letters between my father and his family in those years of his absence. His sisters had informed him of the death of his parents from natural causes. He had never discussed his parents or siblings with me, and I did not ask him about them, not even during our long train ride to Mexico.

For the next ten days my uncle, my father, and I talked about the family, the town, the area, and the living conditions of the local population. We walked the mountain trails while I envisioned what it was like growing up in Zirosto. Over the next fifty years, my memories of the visit resurfaced as I assembled family records and other documents and listened to personal stories by and about migrant farm workers.

Zirosto was little more than a wide horse trail separating clusters of adobe huts with straw-thatched roofs and some houses with wood slatted walls and tin roofs. (As in every village, there were exceptions. A handful of *latifundistas,* absentee land owners, maintained beautifully landscaped mansions as vacation homes to which they came to rest from their stressful exertions in Morelia, the capital of Michoacán, or Mexico, *Distrito Federal.*) Its inhabitants, mostly *mestizo peons* tending agricultural fields for *latifundistas,* had few material goods. To eke out a frugal existence they had to work backyard plots of *maíz* and other vegetables to supplement a necessarily monotonous diet of chicken, frijoles, tortillas, corn tamales, and cornbread.

Birthdays and weddings featured music, drinking, and feasting on various dishes of meat tamales, enchiladas, tostadas, chicken, beef, and pork. Life in Zirosto for the average resident was difficult but tolerable, as evidenced by centuries of acceptance of these conditions with essentially no change in lifestyle.

Zirosto was a racial microcosm of the country. *Mestizos* were in the majority, as they were throughout Mexico four centuries after the arrival of the Spanish conquistadors. The other groups were the purebred Indian descendants of pre-Cortez natives and a much smaller group that traced its unmixed lineage to the Spanish grandees of the colonial era, which ended in the early 1800s.

Although the *mestizo raza* originated in the early 1500s, generations in later centuries continued to receive infusions of Spanish and Indian blood. By the late nineteenth century some *mestizo* brothers, sisters, and first cousins varied in appearance from the classic cinnamon-hued skin, brown eyes, and black-hair types, to the light skin, light-colored eyes, and auburn to blonde hair of the Iberians, with some individuals exhibiting facial characteristics of both groups.

By the twentieth century sociologists had established the subsets, *mestizo-indio* and *mestizo-blanco*. The Mendez-Ynojosa family was a good example of Mexican *mestizo* descent. Unique or predominant Indian characteristics were not observable in their facial or body types. Skin hues were light to slightly cinnamon, and natural hair color varied from light brown to black. A casual observer could stereotype them into the *mestizo-blanco* category without the necessity of a scientific basis to support that classification.

My father and his brother were of the same general appearance, only slightly cinnamon in skin color, and facial features that would have placed them among the conquistadors of the 1500s, despite their dark hair and brown eyes (and a voluntary absence of beards). Their sisters could easily have "passed" for descendants of Spanish grandees in body shape, hair, and skin color.

Formal schooling for Mexican children in outlying villages was generally not available. The Mendez siblings, like their friends and neighbors, learned to read and write the Spanish language at infrequent, informal classes conducted by itinerant teachers who may have had a formal education at a school in a larger town. The adult Natividad's education could be considered the equivalent of that of a public school third grader.

The Mendez children led a hard life, working the agricultural fields alongside adults, gathering and cutting branches for fuel from outlying forest areas, and taking on one-time tasks for a few *centavos* whenever the opportunity arose. The limits on their diet (nutritional value of food, selectivity, and volume) prevented full development of body types. Natividad at full growth weighed no more than 120 pounds, with a height of five feet, five inches. Although he was part of a youthful group with a swelling sense of frustration that chafed at the limitations of life in a Mexican village, he had attempted an escape but found that the harder life of the *betabel* was not an acceptable solution.

"*Oye!* When will we reach the border?" asked my father's newly met traveling companion, who was also from Michoacán.

He was one of several declared migrant farm workers who had banded together for protection over short distances on their way to the United States.

"*Pronto,*" he replied as the weather-beaten bus squeaked, groaned, and coughed the last few miles of its journey to the Mexico-Texas border. "And there will not be any immigration problems."

He was no longer apprehensive after learning earlier in the week that this time he did not have to become a *mojado.* Restrictions on immigration had been lifted and formerly "wetback" migrants no longer had to swim or wade across the Rio Grande to enter the United States at the Texas border.

Waiting in line to enter the checkpoint, Natividad thought back to the events of the past few weeks. He had left Los Reyes on foot after spending hours trying unsuccessfully to hop a train or bus. The next few weeks were repetitive—on foot for hours, hitching a ride between cities on a truck or two heaped with cargo varying from vegetables and fruit to pigs, chickens, scrap metals, and lumber, or sneaking aboard a train or bus making short intercity runs.

Some days he was able to get part-time jobs clearing brush and cleaning up at construction sites, earning just enough for food and used clothing, but not enough for transportation. Nights, he slept mainly in the open or wherever he could find cover from the rain and heavy dews, sometimes spending a fair night's sleep in a shack offered by sympathetic farmers who had only slightly better living accommodations for themselves. Trying to keep clean was difficult. An occasional well helped. He took a dip in a stream at every opportunity, always needed after the sun's rays and the resulting heavy sweat mixed with the road dust to form a thin coating on his skin.

Food availability was literally catch-as-catch-can. He fished in rivers, small lakes, or even streams, where crayfish were plentiful. He plucked ripe fruit from trees near the road. He worked for a few tacos to give him enough strength to continue his pilgrimage. It was a journey to the promised land of life one step above abject poverty, waxing stoop labor and other demeaning jobs, and unhealthy living conditions. And yet it promised hope—hope that did not exist in Zirosto.

As he had done on an earlier trip, seeking work in the *betabel,* he moved in a generally northeast direction. He traveled to and through small and medium-sized cities and crossed the Sierra Madre Oriental mountains wearing only thin cotton clothing and *huaraches.* Exposed to the bone-chilling cold of ten-thousand-foot-elevations, he hurriedly descended to the steaming hot Gulf of Mexico littoral, heading for the Rio Grande.

Natividad walked across the bridge into Texas and did not look back.

※

My mother, Felícitas Silva, was born in Puruandiro, Michoacán, a beautiful mountain village whose calm and peaceful air masked the reality of the harsh life of its inhabitants. Her parents, María Tovar and Juan Silva, had two other children, Jesus, the older sister, and Manuel, her brother. The Silva-Tovar family had a lifestyle typified by that of the Mendez-Ynojosa family in Zirosto, and by hundreds of other Michoacán families.

María Tovar raised her family through perilous times caused by lack of funds attributed to Juan Silva's alcoholism and his resulting inability to provide financial support for his family. She made and enforced difficult decisions without depending on him to play his role as the traditionally designated head of the Mexican family. María saw no future in trying to keep the family together under the circumstances.

She told her children, *"Bueno, niños,* we have to consider leaving Puruandiro for *El Norte."*

My aunt, Tía Jesus, had married Agapito Aguilar, who made extended trips to work at odd jobs and on farms in various states of the southwestern United States. Like many young Mexicans in similar straits, he sent most of his earnings to feed and clothe his family in Puruandiro.

My maternal grandparents left Puruandiro for the United States with their unmarried children, Manuel and Felícitas, at approximately the same time as my father left Zirosto.

CHAPTER TWO

❋ ❋ ❋

Texas

My father took over much of the narration from his brother, telling us about the *betabel* and his life in Texas.

"*Sí*. There is work in the *betabel* and on the railroad," replied strangers whenever he asked them about employment possibilities.

He also inquired about *colonias* where people from Michoacán might be found, figuring that even if he did not run into friends, at least he would feel comfortable living among those with similar backgrounds. Reminded that many of them lived near Houston, he started out for that city, determined to get a job as soon as possible.

It was true that the job situation was promising for unskilled migrants who did not speak English. They were needed by the railroads to work in maintenance departments as track laborers. Sugar beet companies and other southwestern agricultural interests had seasonal shortages of field workers, and heavy industry was highly dependent on laborers for dirty and hazardous duties in the manufacture of metal products. World War I was the motivating factor behind the loosened enforcement of immigration regulations by the federal government. Preparation for and subsequent participation in the war effort by United States citizens created shortages in certain occupations, and concomitant employment opportunities for farm workers and laborers from Mexico.

Peons and other indigents arriving in Texas grouped with relatives, friends, and even strangers claiming to be from the same Mexican town or state. They lived in hovels under deplorable sanitary conditions, sometimes worse than those of the villages they had left. The wages, not high by United States

9

standards but considerably higher than those of Mexico, encouraged them to remain. In 1919 my father arrived in Colorado County, where he met a group of Michoacán families living outside Columbus, a town about one hundred miles west of Houston. They helped him get a temporary farm job and a bunk in an old barn that the owner maintained essentially as sleeping quarters for transient male workers during the growing season.

After going through a winter without a steady income, Natividad decided to join the northward flow of *betabeleros* in the spring. He contacted a broker (someone with an added duty who had worked his way up from migrant-worker status) with an established oral contract with a midwestern grower. They were to work an entire season for a lump sum, to be paid in installments during the growing season. It was expected that they would return to a home base in Texas after harvesting the crops.

Single males started the trip jammed into a truck with wood plank seats and a tarpaulin cover. They were transported through four or five states, stopping only for gasoline, sandwiches or tacos, and water. Urination stops were not even considered—as the need arose, one had only to work his way to the locked tailgate and spray the highway accordingly.

The truck ended its journey at a sugar beet farm in Iowa. The workers were herded into a barrack-type building, actually an old barn containing rows of bunks made of wooden frames with canvas strips for bedsprings; mattresses in the form of used blankets, comforters, and quilts were obtained from charitable organizations or good-hearted persons. Most workers did not require mats. They had no problem sleeping on cardboard placed on the canvas strips. It was a step above the arrangements they'd had in Mexico, sleeping on the floor.

The work was as expected—a hoe with a sharpened cutting edge and an eighteen-inch handle was used to thin out a long, thick row of young sugar beet plants, leaving one or two of the sturdiest plants standing roughly twelve inches apart. A worker stooped and used one hand to swing the hoe in a downward, slicing, digging motion while simultaneously pulling aside the destroyed plants with the other hand. He then shuffled sideways, without straightening, repeating the sequence in that fashion until he reached the end of the row. Inexperienced workers straightened up from time to time to massage their aching back muscles and remove a flap of skin from a punctured blister on the hand wielding the hoe; the sharp sting caused by sweat pouring over the exposed under-skin was stoically endured without expression to avoid giving satisfaction to workers who yelled macho taunts. "*Maricón.* Queer."

Within a few days strengthened back muscles and calluses allowed them to keep pace with the other workers and finish a row without pausing.

After completing the winnowing phase of a contracted tract of sugar beet plantings, the workers performed agricultural tasks at other locations in nearby areas for three or four weeks. By that time the sugar beet plants had grown strong enough to sustain another pass by workers, whose job now was to remove fast growing weeds that absorbed moisture and nutrients from the soil around the plants. The stooped position was assumed and the sugar beet shuffle started once more, this time concentrating on weeds instead of beets.

At the end of the summer growing season the sugar beet plants were pulled out of the ground, the leafy tops cut off, and the underground tubers placed in baskets that were dumped into a trailer for transport to the sugar beet processing plant. The workers began to discuss whether to return to Texas or to remain in the Midwest. They were aware that in Texas they would have to compete for scarce winter jobs with long-time residents and newly arrived Mexican immigrants. Some of them had acquired an improved knowledge of the English language and had made contacts during successive summers, which emboldened them to consider venturing into a different environment where, they believed, better opportunities awaited them.

My father did not see his personal situation as clearly as others saw theirs. After his participation in the *betabel* several years earlier, he had decided that it was not a life that he cared to live. During both trips he became friends with migrant families and closely observed the way they lived.

Housing was little more than an abandoned shack or unused barn, with an entire family cooking, eating, and sleeping in the same room; sometimes, several families shared a house, one family to a room, with a common kitchen and bath (in both instances the family size sometimes ran as high as eight persons). A family established a charge account at the nearest general store for minimal purchases of groceries and household items.

Clothing was strictly hand-me-downs or used clothes, which entered the family's wardrobe as donations by local families and charities. A strong odor of rancid leaf lard (used for cooking) permeated the house, competing with the strong smell of urine-soaked mattresses drying during the day, only to be soaked again by children at night. It was not uncommon for both children and adults to have head lice. Periodically, older children were given the task of hammering away at bedsprings to knock off lice and ticks bloated with blood. Adults had the continuing task of removing lice from children's hair with a fine-tooth comb, which also removed strands of hair from squirming, protesting little bodies.

Food consisted of minimum essentials: wheat flour tortillas, because *maíz* was not readily available in the Midwest, pinto beans, small portions of scrambled eggs, chicken in several prepared forms (all designed to stretch out the chicken), and steer brains, tripe, lungs, and tongue from a nearby slaughterhouse that ordinarily discarded these by-products. Generous use of chile hot sauce fooled the palate into savoring each meal. On festive occasions several dishes were added to the diet. *Posole* was a delicious thick soup containing bits of pork, garbanzos, oregano, carrots, beans, and Iowa corn. *Menudo* was a tasty dish of fried beef tripe prepared with a spicy shredded meat sauce. Tostadas were fried cold tortillas smeared with a mashed refried bean spread, sprinkled with chopped lettuce, tomato, and onion, and topped with the ever-present chile sauce. A pastry called *buñuelos* was kneaded and rolled in the form of a pancake, deep fried in corn oil, removed after expanding, cooled, and served with a coating of corn syrup or honey.

School-age children of migrant families did not attend classes. In a social atmosphere in which longtime residents considered it a luxury for their children to be educated to and through high school, little support could be expected for a program of compulsory education for children of families they considered temporary residents. It was a situation generally acceptable, and in many cases even desirable, to migrant families who felt they needed the children to work in the fields with the adults.

My father decided to return to Texas.

❈

Traveling in a less crowded truck at a more leisurely pace, he carefully reviewed his options. *Betabel* family life did not appeal to him. The continuing chaotic political conditions extant throughout Mexico effectively eliminated the possibility of his returning to his native country. The most attractive alternative was to start a new life in the United States.

Arriving in Colorado County, he rented part of a room from a family originally from Michoacán and started to make the rounds of industrial and commercial firms, looking for any kind of employment. He learned that the nation was in a series of economic ups and downs following the cessation of hostilities of World War I, and that although many companies were reducing employee levels, others were hiring because their particular business opportunities were increasing.

Southern Pacific Railroad (SPRR) was hiring laborers; my father started to work for the railroad in 1920 in its Section Maintenance Department in the town of Glidden, near Columbus, the county seat. The work consisted of cleaning the roundhouse area and picking up trash along the maintenance spur right-of-way leading to the main line. They also performed equipment maintenance tasks, replaced deteriorated railroad ties, and laid track as gandy dancers (a pair of workers swinging heavy hammers in a tightly coordinated series of blows split seconds apart, driving railroad spikes through rail holding plates into wooden ties—the rhythmic movement of wrists, arms, shoulders, and hips evocative of tango dancers performing the scissors leg movement in which the slightest uncoordinated hesitation can lead to disaster).

My father was satisfied with the direction his life was taking, especially with the way his social life was developing. As a bachelor he had plenty of time after work to attend gatherings of friends at birthday parties, patriotic Mexican fiestas, religious observances, and the inevitable cantinas. He noticed that some migrant families preferred to stay year-round in Texas rather than leave each year in the spring and return in the fall, even though it was economically more feasible to participate in the *betabel* each year. Family income of *betabeleros* often exceeded the annual income of a year-round resident. He thought seriously of starting a family and settling down in Texas.

He became a close friend of the Juan Silva and María Tovar family who had arrived recently from Michoacán. He was attracted to sixteen-year-old Felícitas, who was very pretty, with classic cinnamon-hued skin, long, straight, black hair, and beautiful, expressive, brown eyes. She had been raised in the traditional Mexican manner—under close maternal supervision to ensure that she would be a ready, virginal housewife for a closely examined potential husband. The attraction between Felícitas and Natividad did not go unnoticed; the furtive glances, the half-smiles, and the brightening of personality when in each other's presence could not be covered up during their otherwise formal interactions. Natividad and Felícitas were married in Saint Matthias Catholic Church in Columbus, Texas, on December 25, 1920.

The Southern Pacific Railroad provided housing to its Maintenance Department employees in the form of old, unused boxcars moved to the Glidden yards. The cars were modified by cutting rectangular holes in the walls for windows, and the tenants were permitted to build temporary covered patios with used lumber, saplings, and tarpaulins. They created a front yard and children's play area by leveling the embankment and planting flowering bushes. Families suffered from the unrelenting winter cold without sufficient heat in

Standing in the foreground are my father, Natividad, and two unidentified friends; seated is my mother, Felícitas, holding my brother, Joe. In the background is the modified railroad boxcar in which they lived in Glidden, Texas, in 1922. *Mendez family archives.*

the boxcars; in summer, the stupefying heat of a Texas sun beat down on and blistered the painted roofs and sides of their boxcar homes. But, overall, living conditions were much better than those of migrant families in the *betabel.*

Natividad and Felícitas moved into a boxcar home and started a family. My brother, Joe, was born nine months later, our sister, Mary, was born almost exactly one year later, and twin sisters, Josie and Jessie, were born sixteen months after that. The family was beginning to take root in Texas with four American-citizen children. Mexico appeared to be developing a "Cheshire Cat" look in the Mendez fortunes, and even its permanent smile was beginning to fade.

By early 1925 the fluctuating national economy continued to create pockets of recession and rising prosperity in various regions of the country. The railroads and Colorado County were no exception to the rise and fall of profits and employment. SPRR employees became uneasy about the future. They were also affected by news flowing from the Midwest that industrial firms in Chicago, Detroit, Cleveland, and Pennsylvania were recruiting laborers for their plants. In 1923, they heard that the Bethlehem Steel Company had hired roughly one thousand Mexicans to work in its plant in Bethlehem, Pennsylvania, and in the same year the National Tube Company, an affiliate of U.S. Steel, brought thirteen hundred Mexicans from Texas to work in its plant in Lorain, Ohio. After many discussions, the Silva-Tovar and Mendez families decided to make the move to Lorain, where several Michoacán families had relocated and sent back positive accounts of job opportunities with the Baltimore and Ohio (B&O) Railroad and the National Tube Company. My mother was pregnant again, but they went ahead with a two-step travel plan—take part in the *betabel* for a growing season, then, after the harvest, and with enough funds to complete the one thousand-mile trek, continue on to Lorain and a new life.

Accompanied by my grandmother and her son, Manuel, they went by train to Emmet County, Iowa, to work a sugar beet field. My grandfather, Juan Silva, had abandoned his family, heading for California without notice or further contact. Tía Jesus and her husband, Agapito, had left Puruandiro to join her mother and siblings in Texas. After a short stay there, they left to work the *betabel* in Michigan, en-route to Lorain, Ohio. My first cousin, Isabel, was born in Michigan in a railroad boxcar.

In Iowa, our family lived in a shack near the town of Delivar; María Tovar and Manuel lived nearby, working a separate sugar beet tract. My mother's pregnancy and the sugar beet growth advanced in unison as the summer season waned. Fortunately, the beet topping came first, and my parents decided to wait out the next event, the birth of their child, instead of starting out immediately for Ohio. They counted their few dollars, and my father took on small jobs in the area to set aside the money needed for the trip to Lorain.

CHAPTER THREE

Lorain, Ohio

I was born on October 10, 1925, to Felícitas Silva Mendez and Natividad Ynojosa Mendez in a migrant farm worker's shack near Delivar, Iowa. My father cut and tied my umbilical cord, an incident uncommon in 1925 only to the extent that it was usually performed by a midwife or a woman who had participated in the procedure in the past. My parents were alone as intended. When my mother's labor pains started, the four children were sent to a neighbor's house in anticipation of the event. Our grandmother arrived the next day to care for my mother and the five children. She remained with us after her son, Manuel, married Andrea Garcia, who had accompanied her parents from Texas to Iowa.

Two months later I was baptized in Saint John Catholic Church in Lorain, Ohio. My parents christened me Francisco, a name impossible to retain in our Anglicized Midwest; so, Frank it became, informally at first, then officially when public school administrators decided that "foreign" first names were not permitted on school records. I became aware of my real name at age sixteen when I saw my Iowa birth certificate for the first time.

Lorain, Ohio, when we arrived, was still recovering from the most devastating natural disaster in its history. A major tornado had leveled a large part of the town a year earlier. Arriving in the wake of a tornado in what was to be our hometown, it didn't register with us that this natural disaster was a harbinger of the personal disasters to come. But come they did, in numbers and degree that at times pushed our family to the edge.

Lorain was originally an Indian settlement founded at the mouth of the Black River, whose slowly flowing murky waters carried drainage from the

Ohio highlands into Lake Erie, along with the seeping runoff from the underlying fractured sandstone substrata formed in an earlier age as the bed of a disappeared ocean. It was an ideal location for a village, but by the 1920s the Indians were long gone and Lorain had become part of the heavy industrial complex stretching from Toledo on the western shore of Lake Erie to Cleveland (approximately thirty miles east of Lorain) and beyond. The local high school anthem best described Lorain as the place "where the coal and iron meet," the coal coming by rail from the Pennsylvania mines and the iron ore by lake freighter from the Minnesota Mesabi Range. In the mills of the National Tube Company, the raw materials were converted into malleable iron and alloyed steel tubing and steel bars.

My father started working as a laborer in the blast furnace section of the company in December 1925. The company had been in operation since 1895 as the Lorain Steel Company when it was built and operated by Tom Johnson, who went on to become famous as a progressive congressman and mayor of Cleveland. He sold the company in 1898 to the Federal Steel Company (predecessor to U. S. Steel).

The National Tube Company ran along the west and south banks of the Black River, from its mouth to the end of South Lorain, a distance of roughly five miles. Its heavy mill operations were located in South Lorain, separated by the Baltimore and Ohio Railroad tracks from the rest of the city. South Lorain was "across the tracks" figuratively as well, the least desirable "real estate address" in Lorain. It was a polyglot of first and second generation immigrant families who, for the most part, depended directly or indirectly on the steel mill and its supporting industries for their livelihood. In many homes English was a second language, or at best a close tie with Hungarian, Italian, Spanish, Russian, Polish, Czech, Lithuanian, Slovak, Greek, Romanian, Croatian, Serbian, German, or Ukrainian.

During the day, a perpetual haze formed from the fine mill ash that hung suspended in the air or fell gently onto rooftops, lawns, and streets. The glow of the blast furnace, the white-hot stream of molten steel pouring into the open hearth, and the explosion of light from the mouth of the huge Bessemer retort as compressed air was injected into the molten mass, lighted the night for hours at a time.

The smoldering presence of the National Tube Company loomed in the background of this "village," both physically and emotionally. Its industrial operations spewed steam and smoke and dust and ash and noise; hundreds of squeaking, clanging railroad cars, loaded with coal, entered the factory grounds daily, clanging even louder after dumping their loads at the ovens where the coal was baked into coke; the roar of the blast furnaces followed as the burning coke and iron ore were mixed with limestone and smelted, later emerging as steaming casts of pig iron; the open hearth operations, next in line, remelted the pig iron, added alloys to the molten lake, and, in conjunction with the Bessemer process, produced the steel blooms, huge casts of red-hot solid steel; on moved the blooms, on heavy duty rollers, into the rolling mills where they were forced under tremendous pressure into powerful dies that converted them into bars and flat strips of various widths and thickness; in the pipe mills, the still malleable steel strips were formed and seam welded into pipe, or extruded through mandrils and dies, emerging as seamless steel tubing to be loaded and shipped on railroad flatcars to distributors of steel products.

One has only to visualize the degree of human involvement in the operation of the steel mills in the preautomated, precomputerized, prerobotics age to conclude that large numbers of laborers and semiskilled workers were required to produce the final products of the National Tube Company. The workers spent the greater part of their lives in South Lorain raising children to replace them in the mills.

Most of the workers lived in a one-square-mile area south of the skyline-dominating smokestacks of the company's mills and plants. Our first home was just outside South Lorain, but it was not long before we moved within walking distance of the Vine Avenue employee gate, one of three entry points along the tube company's fenced boundary. The four block rectangular parcel just outside the gates was where most of the Mexican workers and their families lived, mainly in multifamily buildings, some of which could realistically be called tenements.

Although there was no formally recognized geographical barrio, Mexicans and Mexican Americans were closely united in a de facto barrio by the bonds of our poverty, as well as the Spanish language and ethnic rituals of the Catholic Church. We visited one another's families, making little distinction between relatives and friends, formed social clubs, participated in patriotic Mexican festivals and observances, and generally shared one another's misfortunes. The closeness and mutual support did not deter us from mixing with members of other ethnic groups. Friendships also developed with non-Mexicans, mostly neighbors and schoolmates. It was a time of comparatively friendly community relations, despite the strains of sharply contrasting backgrounds and social status.

My mother had given birth to five children in four years, and her health had begun to deteriorate; she was diagnosed as having a tubercular kidney. Home remedies were attempted, one of which consisted of pressing the mouth of a heated drinking glass over the kidney area. This created a partial vacuum that was supposed to draw the "badness" out of the kidney. Felícitas Silva Mendez was twenty-four years old when she died. I was two and one-half years old and have no memory of her beyond anecdotal remembrances of my grandmother and Tía Jesus, my mother's sister.

Through the years I have studied pictures of my mother in her late teens. My cinnamon-hued skin and straight black hair closely resemble hers and sharply contrast the light features of my siblings and father. Ironically, I have not missed her in the sense of feeling pain from the loss of a deceased parent. Grandmother María Tovar, with her constant demonstration of love and caring for her grandchildren, adequately compensated for her daughter's absence, at least in our eyes and minds. We called Grandmother "Mama" for the rest of her life, and she tacitly encouraged it by failing to correct us. In so doing, she showed a deeper psychological insight than those who made the simplistic comment, "She's your grandmother, not your mother." She instinctively sensed the desperate need of five adolescents to identify with a mother figure, and in this case the appropriate one was readily available and able to fill that void. María Tovar could not read, write, or speak English, nor could she read or write Spanish. Yet she consistently demonstrated more intelligence than others with diplomas and degrees.

While our mother lay bedridden the last few months of her life, and during the years following her death, Grandmother assumed the nursing and mothering obligations. She ran the house with an impressive strength and imposing character to keep five young children alive on limited funds from our father's work. It was more of a challenge than that of her earlier life in Mexico and Texas, where she had managed a home for her three children and an irresponsible alcoholic husband. In our case, my father was a steady worker who had only a few drinks a week, but their in-law relationship was irremediably strained because of strongly held, but differing views on the degree of a parent's dedication to the care and upbringing of the children.

Their differences brought on a family crisis when my father placed four of us in the Lorain County Orphanage; my sister Josie was in the hospital after being diagnosed with infantile paralysis (later called poliomyelitis). I was six years old at the time and remember very little of our stay at the orphanage, aside from a group sing-along about someone leaving the Red River Valley

My grandmother, Maria Tovar, in a photo taken in the mid-1940s.
Mendez family archives.

and being in a large room with other children where my sister held my hand
as if to lead me to a seat. I retain a good feeling for the attendants and the
kindness they bestowed on us, but I can recall no specific incidents to support
the origins of that feeling. My sisters confirm my understanding of our stay in
the orphanage; it was not the child-abusing chamber of horrors frequently
depicted in movies and lurid novels.

My grandmother obviously did not agree with my father's decision; she
approached anyone she thought could help her get us out of the orphanage
and finally accomplished it after our stay of four months. The agreement
with our father was that she would set up a home and raise his children with
his limited financial support. He would live in a nearby boarding house and
be available when needed. Grandmother never requested his presence or his

intercession beyond sending one of the children to pick up the biweekly stipend at the boarding house—my chore at around ten years of age. He also gave each of his five children a twenty-five cent allowance, which we looked forward to; my four siblings always anxiously awaited me as I stepped into the house. A quarter could buy a soda, a chocolate candy bar, and a grab bag of candy, or a ticket to a Saturday movie matinee and a small bag of popcorn.

The money our father sent was not enough for rent, food, clothing, medicine, and other incidentals involved in raising a family of five children. Mama had no other source of income beyond what she could earn washing and ironing clothes for the many Mexican bachelors living in the neighborhood. She managed to keep us alive, together, and functioning as a family under almost impossible circumstances brought on by the Great Depression of the 1930s and its pervasive negative economic influence on families at all social levels.

There were several Mexican couples who helped us with donations of used clothing, furniture, utensils, and maintenance work on the various apartments we rented. They were real friends who readily gave advice and assistance, impressed with Mama's ability to overcome so many obstacles without complaining about her status in life. They could see her dedication to our well-being. When Josie had several foot operations over an eight-year period, which required many lengthy hospital stays or confinement in bed at home, she was always lovingly attended by Mama.

Joe began to have petit mal and grand mal epileptic seizures at the age of eleven. They could occur at any time, sometimes in public. He would suddenly freeze and stare fixedly ahead, then lose control of the muscles that held him in an upright position. Eventually he had to be accompanied by Mama or a sibling whenever he left the house. We learned to identify the early symptoms of a grand mal seizure—sudden cessation of activity, rapidly blinking eyes, and a slight turning of his head while slowly licking his lips. We were usually able to guide him into a sitting position, then, as the violence of the seizure spread-eagled him on the floor, cushion his head with our thighs or arms, thereby limiting the injurious bruises to his flailing knees, arms, and elbows. The seizures lasted no more than twenty seconds. Petit mal seizures lasted a few seconds, identifiable only by the same facial expressions and some unintelligible words.

When Joe was sixteen years old, his lower lip and jaw were gashed to the bone when he fell and hit a sharp-edged brick. After leading him to his bed, we called the neighborhood general practitioner. On a house call, he examined Joe and said, "I have to close the cut with needle and thread. I do not

The Mendez children. From the left, Jessie, Josie, Mary, Joe, and me. We were living in one of the several different houses we occupied in South Lorain during the early 1930s. *Mendez family archives.*

plan to administer an anesthetic because it might cause permanent damage." He looked at me and added, "Hold his hands firmly. I am sure the pain will cause him to react and try to interfere with the sewing operation." The open gash stretched from just below the midpoint of his lower lip and downward to the left, ending on the underside of the jawbone. It was at least three inches long and half-an-inch deep, with a quarter-inch separation between the long sides of the cut. During the operation, blood seeped and dripped onto the towel placed under his head. Each time the doctor inserted the needle into and through both sides of the cut, Joe gasped, moaned, and tried to grab the doctor's hand. At least twice my brother broke free of my grasp, causing the physician to hesitate, stare at me, and say, "Hold his hands!"

For many years thereafter, the long raised scar tissue on Joe's jaw reminded us of the pain and suffering he bore quietly. He had to drop out of school in the sixth grade because school authorities feared his seizures were disrupting classes. He had done well in his studies, and on his own initiative he read our textbooks and made notebooks of the homework exercises until he could no longer keep up with the advancing grade levels. Tutoring assistance was out of the question—it simply did not exist in our "society." Joe and Mama spent each day together in a bond that helped them immeasurably to face the difficult years ahead.

My sister Mary became the acknowledged head of the family even before reaching her teens. Her mature firmness in support of our grandmother helped maintain discipline in a family that needed a sense of order to merely exist in the chaotic life of the Great Depression. It was not easy to assume that role in the face of minor rebellions by siblings who did not like being "bossed around" by a peer. Gradually, the resentment evolved into appreciation as we realized that her demands were based solely on her desire to establish a safe and secure future for all of us.

Initially, I called my sister "Rooster," claiming that she was always crowing; shortly, my admiration for her ability caused me to change the name to Rouge, teasingly drawing out the pronunciation as "ROO-OOZH." She spoke for the family in our dealings with stores, doctors, hospital, schools, civic officials, and other families, Mexican or otherwise. Recalling those days later in life, I do not remember her playing children's games; no dolls, no childhood fantasies—she was an adult while others her age were still growing up. Without her support and implementation of Mama's decisions, the family would probably have disintegrated as a unit.

In the early thirties, after routine medical tests at school, Mama was told by health authorities to place Mary, Jessie, and me in the Pleasant View Sanitarium for examination and observation for tuberculosis. The incident I remember most was a sympathetic nurse counseling me about my wetting the bed at night (the epithet my siblings used when irritated with me was "Skunk").

She asked, "What were you dreaming when it happened?"

I replied, "I don't know. I just wake up when I piss the bed."

Quickly, she responded, "Honey, you should say 'wet' the bed."

She did not ask any more questions.

I had an older roommate who showed me how to blow fuses by sticking the prongs of a hairpin into the holes of a convenience outlet while holding the pin with a handkerchief. He also demonstrated how to avoid walking the "icy" floor of the corridor at night to the central toilet.

He placed a chair in front of the washbasin in our bedroom, and said, "Watch this." He stood on the chair, urinated into the bowl, and made a mad dash back to the bed and slid under the covers. He was very creative, and I was the dunce who was always caught by the nurses when I tried to do the same.

After a stay of three months my sisters and I were released with no symptoms of tuberculosis, and no idea if we had contracted it. In general, I have fond memories of the attendants, even if I cannot remember many specifics of our stay. We had overcome homesickness by trying to meet at every opportunity and were encouraged to do so by workers who helped us arrange the meetings. We were overjoyed when Mama came to take us home, transportation furnished by the same friends who had brought her, Joe, and Josie for visits, and who were always there for emergency transportation.

The girls helped grandmother to wash and iron bachelors' clothes; Joe and I picked up and delivered the clothes. We also took on minor chores for small change from neighbors and storeowners. We roamed the alleys, sorting through trash piles and collecting rags, scrap steel, aluminum, and empty soda and milk bottles. We collected the deposits on the bottles and sold the other materials to junkmen who toured the streets in horse-drawn wagons and paid a few pennies per pound for rags and metals.

Each complete block in South Lorain contained an alley that ran through the middle and separated the rows of houses on either side. Backyard gates emptied into the alley, and because there was no municipal trash removal, residents placed the waste on a pile, sometimes setting it on fire. After a few weeks, the debris expanded behind each residence. It was easy to sit or kneel and pick through a pile of unburned scraps, selecting items to place in a large burlap sack. We did not wear gloves, which resulted in frequent cuts and scratches that we ignored and for which we sometimes suffered the consequences. Infections were easily resolved by dissolving Epsom salts in hot water and applying this to the infected area, then popping the "whitehead" after it surfaced.

Children my age and younger, playing in their backyards, made a game of shouting, "Rag-pickers, Rag-pickers!" They stuck out their tongues at us as we worked our way past their property. Joe acted as if he did not hear them; I winced inwardly and tried to ignore them, but I was ashamed and hurt, and probably showed it. I did not cease to be a rag picker—we needed the money. Months later I met a few of the name callers at elementary school and we became friends, outwardly forgetting the rag picking games. But inside remained the vestiges of something I could not define, at least not then.

There were other putdowns, usually based on my physical appearance. Much of the time I went barefoot from spring to autumn, wore cheap, patched, secondhand clothes, and did not change shirt or trousers for several days. The fact that I had only one or two changes of clothing was no excuse—I actually believed that I was supposed to be like that, in keeping with the expressed "Anglo" view, "That's the way Mexicans live."

I called myself a Mexican, even though I knew I was an American citizen. I cooperated in this inculcation, accepting the not infrequent reference to "dirtymeskins" without challenging its use (in my case, the first two syllables were an accurate description of my deplorable personal hygiene). Some old Hungarians in the neighborhood, who spoke little or no English, called me a phonetic PEE-SOOKEE-MET-SEE-KAHN, and left no doubt that it was intended as a pejorative.

My close friends of Hungarian descent, at my insistence, interpreted the word over-protectively. "Don't let it bother you. You're a good guy, not like other Mexicans."

The irony was that many of the "other Mexicans" my age were held in higher esteem in the barrio than I was. Their parents were hard workers who rented or bought houses in a nice neighborhood; their children dressed in good, clean clothes and were monitored closely for their participation in school and community activities. They had every right and reason to consider themselves "as good as" the *güeros* (a friendly term for non-Mexican whites, also used as a nickname for Mexicans with light complexions and auburn hair).

My sisters and I picked raspberries and currants on nearby fruit farms during the summer months, along with the children of other poor families. Mary was the prime mover in organizing our participation in this endeavor.

"Frank, get up. Time to get ready to go and pick berries," she reminded me early each morning. "Come on, Frank. Hurry up. Get something to eat and let's go."

My grandmother had prepared the usual breakfast of small servings of toast, milk, tortillas, and beans, the last two items served three times a day. The lunch and supper meals were augmented with a meat product (almost always slices of baloney) and one or two vegetables. The portions were small, not very filling, and there were no second servings. I scoured my plate with my last piece of tortilla—dishwashing was a lark.

We walked two blocks to East Thirty-first Street, each of us carrying a lunch of a bean taco and an egg sandwich, and waited with twenty-five or thirty others for the farm trucks to pick us up. The mornings went rapidly. The picked berries went into one-quart baskets, each worth a chit, to be converted to cash at the end of the short workday. After lunch, we worked another hour or so and were driven back to town.

For most of us, the berry-picking sessions were a diversion. We escaped from our normal routines and carried on conversations away from the scrutiny of those of the older generation, who viewed the use of English as a conspiracy to encourage children to abandon the "old ways." My siblings and I spoke English exclusively with each other and with our closest Chicano friends and acquaintances. We also carried on extended conversations in Spanish with older Latinos who would speak English only as a courtesy to *güeros* who did not understand Spanish.

I did not know where I belonged: I could totally assimilate the American culture as represented by books, movies, teachers, and my *güero* friends and acquaintances, or remain preponderantly within the Mexican culture of my grandmother and those of our barrio friends who could not, or would not, change their strongly held views of who they were or where they came from. They were as comfortable in their skins as my American compatriots were in theirs.

Prior to leaving my adolescent years, and without realizing it, I had chosen to be an all-American boy. But I could not jump out of my skin. The mirror made that very clear to me, and subconsciously it fanned, ever so lightly, an ember of indignation and defiance within me.

※

The Great Depression of the 1930s provided the background for the formative years of my life. We lived fully under its influence, as did millions of other Americans. Paradoxically, many of them faced more tragic financial and emotional crises simply because we had no paradise to lose. With hardly any material goods, no earned income, no savings, and no real estate, we had nothing, except perhaps a strong family bond that could not be broken by external influences. It was that bond that guided us through the Depression.

We were placed on "Relief," a form of welfare that only provided government surplus food to indigent families on an irregular basis. At least one of us accompanied Mama on each trip to the storefront government surplus center to pick up and carry whatever foods were being distributed that day. The usual foods, not all available at the same time, were bread, oranges, potatoes, grapefruit, and a terrible-smelling dried meat product that tasted worse than it looked but was never rejected. Charities contributed used clothes. Our father's limited financial support ameliorated the situation but did not substantially alter it. Mama performed miracles to keep us fed, clothed, and warm during the cold Ohio winters.

Our main food staple was *frijoles,* served three times a day, but I never tired of the beans. Between meals I would enter the house and head straight for the kitchen stove, where a pot of refried beans was always at the ready. I'd pick up a tortilla from the small pile beside the stove, lay it on the burner grate, put a lighted match to the orifices of the cast iron burner, and turn on the control knob. After heating the tortilla, I'd scoop up two tablespoons of refried beans, tap them onto the tortilla, and spread half a spoonful of chile sauce over the beans. Licking the spoon, I'd fold over one side of the tortilla and repeat the process, rolling the taco into a cylinder and bending the open bottom as I picked it up and took a huge bite out of the other end. Two or three more bites, and I'd hurry out the kitchen door, leaving a mess for my sisters to clean up, unconcerned about the "there-he-goes-again" looks and raised voices about a spoiled brat. They were correct. I avoided household chores, and they resignedly performed the duties I should have shared. They kept the house spotless and in very fine order, as demanded by Mama.

I did not know at that time that Mama's "softness" toward my participation in household tasks could very well have been due to a Mexican tradition of *mimando* (spoiling, for want of a better translation) the young males of a family. Families in Spanish-speaking countries still consider it unmanly for a young male to sweep and swab floors or wash windows, let alone wash dishes or clothes. In my adolescent and teenage years I gravitated innocently (and willingly) toward that cultural phenomenon and became, in my sisters' words, "a lazy, spoiled kid."

There were a few chores that I did not try to avoid. One task was culling from a one-pound bag of beans the bits of pebbles that had escaped the eyes of the pickers and processors. It took only one chipped tooth to convince me that I could never again eat cooked beans unless I had personally inspected every bag prior to their being cooked. Two other chores were of interest to me. I dug up sassafras roots growing in the woods for Mama's tea, and when we had no spinach plants and could not afford to buy any, I snipped dandelion leaves from the nearby grassland areas. I detected little difference in taste between the cooked spinach and dandelion leaves.

In the mid-thirties, after a succession of moves, we settled into a weather-beaten wooden cottage, built somewhat as an afterthought behind a store on Vine Avenue, a block from the steel-plant gate. The house was hemmed in by the store and the concrete walls of commercial buildings on each side. The rear property line was a high wooden fence, separated from the living quarters by a ten-foot stretch of weeds and trash, which we converted into a garden plot of tomatoes, peppers, carrots, and peas. The only access to the cottage was a narrow walkway between two stores. It provided us with a measure of privacy and a quiet home life, as opposed to the open, unquiet living conditions of four to eight families jammed into a row of multiplex housing units whose front doors were usually left open for children who played unsupervised in the hallways.

Our house consisted of a kitchen with a gas-fired stove, a cold-water sink, and a table for four; a small bedroom barely contained Joe's bunk and mine, with no space for a dresser and no closet (our meager personal possessions were stored in cardboard boxes under the beds); a larger room was partitioned into a living room with a centrally placed, coal burning, pot-bellied cast iron stove, and a sleeping area for Mama and two of my sisters, the third sister using a convertible couch in the living room as a bed; a walk-in storage closet off the kitchen led to a bathroom that had no wash basin, shower, or tub, only a commode. Bathing once a week was the generally accepted custom in Lorain (except for those with "dirty" jobs who could shower at the steel mill). Our family bathed using a large galvanized metal laundry tub. My friends and I gave up the laundry tub routine as teenagers; we took showers three or four times a week at the YMCA prior to using its swimming pool.

I was comfortable with how we lived, primarily because I spent only a few daylight hours in the house. Much of my time was occupied by my favorite activities—school, some minor temporary neighborhood jobs, reading in the book and magazine section of the neighboring drug store after cleaning its floor and basement storage area, and hanging out with close friends of various ethnicities. We engaged in several sports, conducted explorations of abandoned fruit farms and heavily wooded areas, fished (with a makeshift line and hook), and skinny-dipped in remote locations on the Black River, Lake Erie, and a few flooded quarries, returning from these forays with discarded but usable trash, bags of apples, pears, and peaches, or boxes of cherries, blackberries, and mulberries (but no fish). We walked up to ten miles on side roads, along railroad tracks, through woods and open fields, occasionally hitching rides on slow-moving boxcars and trucks. It was a camaraderie without interpersonal restraints—we talked openly about everything from movies, school, books, sports, to girls, the last item discussed in colossal ignorance of the female mind and body.

"That good-looking girl down the block is in the hospital with appendicitis."

"Yeah, her boy friend banged her so hard he ruptured her appendix."

Although unsupervised by adults, we conducted our activities with a healthy respect for the law, represented in the form of a policeman, a fence, an unoccupied house, or an innate acknowledgment of another's legal and moral rights. We were idealists with a slightly romantic bent fostered by movies, comic books, and contact with respected adults. Any deviation from our unspoken rules was usually mixed with a touch of humor, like the time an "old" man, speaking in a European tongue, asked if we would help him clear a large plot of land for a garden.

Dick, who understood his language, said, "Hey, we can probably earn a few dollars."

So we worked several sweaty hours, cutting and pulling up weeds and burning trash. Finished, we gathered expectantly around the man.

Dick interpreted. "He says he has no money, but he'll dance at our weddings."

Louie, the group wit, responded, "Give him our thanks, and tell him we'll dance on his grave."

We left giggling, as we usually did after a biting comment by Louie, knowing that Dick would not do a literal translation.

One had only to emerge from the narrow walkway of our house to feel the Vine Avenue and East Twenty-ninth Street ambience. "Vine and Twenty-ninth" was the symbolic center of a three-by-six-block mini-village, a residential neighborhood with a small commercial strip that ran along Vine Avenue from the steel company's gate at East Twenty-eighth Street to the B&O roundhouse six blocks to the south. Steelworkers passed here, walking firmly toward the gate, while the earlier shift plodded wearily homeward or headed for one of the bar and grill joints for a stress-reducing boilermaker, or two, or three, or more.

Immediately to the north of our Vine Avenue walkway exit was a family owned and operated drugstore containing a soda fountain and a publications section (comic books, magazines, newspapers, and, most important to me, pulp magazines—*The Shadow, The Spider, Operator 5,* and *G-8 and His Battle Aces,* fantasy worlds that I disappeared into for hours at a time). The drugstore anchored the southwest corner of Vine and Twenty-ninth. Across the street on the northwest corner was a dry-goods store that had closed during the Depression, as had at least one other store per block along Vine Avenue.

On the northeast corner was a family-owned dairy that served much of South Lorain. It had a stable of three or four horses that pulled the home delivery wagons; these were a delight for those of us who, raised on city streets, found the touch of horseflesh a thrill. Early each morning, trucks picked up the classic five-gallon containers of milk from nearby farms. The milk was pasteurized in the dairy, then sold and delivered in glass quarts, the nonhomogenized cream floating to the top.

An abandoned gas station occupied the southeast corner opposite the dairy. It was our open-air clubhouse, a place to play catch or wait for a "quorum" of our age group to show up for the gang walk to Whittier Junior High School four blocks away. Each morning I looked forward to joining other teenagers for our walk-and-talk sessions. I initiated the conversation. "Well, what are we going to do today after school, John?"

"Umm, don't know. Maybe we can hitch a ride to Central Park to watch the football game between Whittier and Hawthorne for the junior high championship," replied John.

"Gee, I don't know about that," I said. "I haven't been following them. None of us has ever tried out for football. We're too small. Here comes Pancho. Let's hear what he has to say."

"Hi, what are you guys planning?" asked Pancho.

"Umm, we've talked about the football game at Central Park. Any ideas?" said John.

"I want to see the softball game tonight between the *Club Ideal* and a team from uptown. Joe Mendoza will be pitching and Benny Zamora will catch. Maybe I can get into the game as a sub. How about tomorrow?" asked Pancho.

I said, "I can't go anywhere with you guys tomorrow. It's Saturday, and my sister tells me that I have to go with her to a meeting of *La Sociedad Mutualista Mejicana*. They are meeting to plan our participation in the *Cinco de Mayo* fiesta for next year. You know, the Fifth of May pageant. She has to organize her Mexican girls club to get boys and girls to dance the *Jarabe Tapatío* in *charro* and *china poblana* clothes. She says I have to be a *charro*."

John closed the conversation with, "I guess that takes care of our weekend activities."

East and west on East Twenty-ninth Street were a few multifamily residential buildings and many well-kept single family houses with wide front porches, the standard porch swing, and neat lawns for quiet family activities. Halfway down the block was the Neighborhood House, a settlement house supported by private donations and municipal grants. The social workers encouraged residents of various ages to organize practical projects aimed at making us good American citizens. They conducted classes in very basic English for newly arrived immigrants of all ages, guided us into forming young men's and women's social clubs, provided volunteer teachers to help Chicanos learn correct Spanish grammar, and conducted music lessons with the intention of forming an orchestra. They also made "house calls" on reclusive residents to determine the community's needs. Two of the social workers had studied and worked at Chicago's famous Hull House; they were as dedicated to their professions as nuns and ministers are to their respective callings. Two of them remained single and spent the major part of their careers at the South Lorain settlement house; many of us remembered them fondly through the years.

There was much activity on Vine Avenue during the day. Housewives carried or pulled shuffling children to the drugstore, the small A&P grocery store, or their mother's house, occasionally pausing to chat with a friend or a shop owner sweeping the sidewalk in front of his store.

Here also walked and skipped the energetic adolescents going to or coming from Lincoln Elementary School. They slowed down and moved cautiously to the street edge of the sidewalk as they passed the gypsy family's fortune-casting store and living quarters, sneaking side glances at children their age dressed in East European gypsy clothes (their usual dress, not a fashion show supporting a staged production).

The other streets intersecting Vine Avenue were similar to East Twenty-ninth Street in appearance. We lived on East Thirtieth Street for a short time in one of six identical red brick multiplex houses. My earliest memory is about an incident that occurred there when I was five years old. I was playing in the backyard of our building when I noticed a horse-drawn wagon on the street passing our unit. I ran between the buildings to the street, following the horse and wagon, enthralled by the sight. Suddenly, I noticed that I was in a strange country, not one in which I was always surrounded by red brick buildings. I looked back, saw the buildings a short distance away and started toward them. I entered the walkway between two buildings and found an unfamiliar backyard. Frightened, I ran back to the street and entered another walkway only to find another different yard. Terrified, I started to cry; a stranger quietly took me by the hand and led me to my house. I was overjoyed to see familiar surroundings. An amateur psychologist might conclude that even then I did not know where I belonged.

Between the steel mill perimeter fence and East Twenty-eighth Street was a heavily wooded area where we held our coming of age rituals—gagging on corn silk cigarettes, and roasting potatoes and ears of corn "pilfered" from the overproducing gardens of an owner who looked the other way, and who knew we knew he looked the other way. His son admitted sheepishly that his father always laughed after yelling at us the night before, which undercut our wild stories of hearing shots and pellets whizzing overhead. In the woods we conducted energetic "King of the Hill" rumbles with perceived rivals from other neighborhoods who happened to "invade" our turf. The worst injuries were an accidental bloody nose or scraped knee or elbow. We would meet again the next day in junior high school gym class where we faced yesterday's adversaries, this time as opposing teammates. The game and gym class usually ended with joking and friendly roughhousing that eventually led to closer friendships at the high school level.

Our first six years of public school were spent at Lincoln Elementary School, a short walk from our house. The teachers were competent educators, dedicated but grossly unappreciated—financially by the parents, and emotionally by several students in each class. The boys tried too hard to emulate our fictional heroes, Tom Sawyer and Huckleberry Finn, and I personally made life difficult for teachers by disrupting classes with inane, inappropriate comments, trying to show off my broad, but superficial reading knowledge. Of course, I was appropriately disciplined by the principal's favorite teaching technique, an eighteen-inch paddle that quickly caught my attention, and my tears, but did not eliminate a hidden rebelliousness, fed by observations of social elitism and racial injustice.

My assimilation into the American way of life had its rocky beginnings. Fortunately for me, my challenges did not rise to Heathcliffian heights of anger and frustration.

❊ ❊ ❊

CHAPTER FOUR

Growing Up Chicano

By the time I was ready for high school, I had managed to control my intemperate outbursts in class, thanks in great part to the influence of Miss Lester, my seventh grade English and homeroom teacher. She noted that I needed attention, and she patiently worked with me to channel my energies toward goals that I had never considered to be within my reach. I became an honor student and my social awareness improved. She was the model teacher whom the student never forgets—the teacher whose reward is in knowing that she contributed to a positive change in the life of a student who appeared to be headed toward a troublesome future.

The first day in English class she announced, "This semester we will read the *Odyssey*. Does anyone know what it is about?"

The class did not respond.

She asked, "Did you not read the *Iliad* in the sixth grade?"

Most students stared at her without expression. I raised my hand to a surprised Miss Lester, who was looking at a "Mexican" kid with unkempt hair, an old wrinkled shirt, patched trousers, and badly worn, dirty shoes.

She glanced at her seating chart and said, "Yes, Frank?"

I blurted out, "The *Iliad* is about the Trojan War between ancient Greeks, and the *Odyssey* covers the adventures of Ulysses after the war, when he's returning to his home and his wife, PENNY-LOAP."

A girlish titter arose and subsided quickly with Miss Lester's look of displeasure at the behind-the-hand whispering of "Penelope."

She looked in my direction and said, "Class, I'm glad we have someone who can help us understand the more difficult parts of the *Odyssey*."

As the class ended, Miss Lester motioned me to her desk and said, "Frank, I have a tough job ahead of me preparing my semester files. I have students from three elementary schools and a few students who transferred from other cities. Will you help me set up the files?"

In the space of a few weeks I went from Peck's Bad Boy (a fictional character's name applied to me by an exasperated sixth grade teacher) to Teacher's Pet. My personal appearance and manners improved. I was on the Honor Roll most grading terms, receiving several "As" despite my inability to, or lack of interest in, developing good study habits. I was a totally undisciplined student, a voracious but undiscriminating reader with little regard for school assignments, preferring to immerse myself in a vicarious world of my favorite authors, subjects, and characters. I applied myself only to subjects that I found interesting or challenging, coasting through the other subjects with "Bs" or "Cs." I had no problem with tests; I skimmed textbooks at my own speed, listened attentively to lectures and classroom discussions, and recalled with little effort much of the material during tests and exams.

In the ninth grade, students were placed in the college preparatory or general studies curricula. Mexican Americans, blacks, and children of Eastern European descent were routinely assigned to General Studies unless a parent objected. Few did. *Güeros* with Anglo-Saxon last names were asked if their parents wanted them to be assigned to the College Prep Course. It required two years of Latin, two years of another foreign language, Algebra II, geometry, trigonometry, and chemistry or physics. All students attended the other classes; a General Studies student was permitted to attend a college prep class as an elective, if he met the prerequisites.

The selection criterion for assignment to school courses was loosely patterned after a Lorain custom of using a person's nationality to pigeonhole him into various social groupings. Whites with Anglo-Saxon last names were called Americans despite the fact that they might not be citizens. Mexican Americans and other citizens with Eastern European last names were referred to as Mexicans, Poles, Russians, Serbs—that is, by the nationality of their parents or grandparents. Students or parents generally did not challenge the validity of the practice. It was understood throughout Lorain that when "nationality" was requested, the nationality of a male ancestor was supposed to be reported, except for Anglo-Saxon whites. The nationality of a black was Negro.

I was aware of other discriminatory practices. Blacks were not permitted to use the YMCA swimming pool with whites and Mexican Americans— they could use it only on Tuesdays and Thursdays. A black male could not dance with a white or "brown" female in public, and even friendly body contact raised eyebrows.

The group of Chicanos and *güeros* I regularly mixed with (our gang, if you will) did not include a black. There were only three black families in our four-block mini-village, all of them living several blocks from Vine and Twenty-ninth. The junior high school class of which I was a member consisted of three homerooms, and included three blacks. I felt a sort of kinship with them, a view common among Chicanos in the barrio when associating with blacks—and yet there was little social intermingling. There appeared to be an invisible wall separating us after school hours—with few attempts on either side to remove the barrier.

One day, several of my friends and I decided to go swimming in a quarry on the outskirts of town. As we were passing the house of a black classmate, I saw him sitting on the porch.

I called out, "Hi, Robert. How ya doing?"

He replied, "OK, where are you guys headed?"

I answered, "To the quarry. Going swimming. Come along."

The others waved a "come on" motion. He hesitated a second, nodded, and joined us on the long walk.

At the quarry we stripped, yelled, and jumped into the water, except for Robert. He had also stripped, but stood quietly on the top sandstone ledge of the quarry, which was underwater, but only two feet lower than the level of the ground (like all flooded quarries in the area, this one was composed of stratified sandstone walls with various levels projecting from each wall).

We guessed that he was waiting for his body to adjust to the temperature of the water, and we shouted, "It's OK. Jump in!"

Robert dove into the water and came up gasping and thrashing. It was obvious that he did not know how to swim; we dove in and pulled him back to the top ledge. A few minutes later he had regained his composure; we dressed and left the quarry. By the time we reached his house, we were all joking and ribbing him good-naturedly.

After we left Robert's house, we realized that we had made a serious mistake by not asking Robert if he knew how to swim. We assumed that all teenage boys living in the vicinity of Lake Erie, the Black River, and the numerous quarries knew how to swim. The incident was an example of how members of one race can fail to understand that another race may not have the advantages considered commonplace by other races. Blacks were denied equal opportunity to use the YMCA swimming pool, all of the Lake Erie beaches (save one small isolated beach), the Black River landings, and most of the quarries. We should not have been surprised to learn that Robert did not know how to swim.

I worked the summer nights of 1941 as a "tray boy" at a drive-in root beer stand, and developed a crush on a *güera* who came there frequently. Apparently, I misunderstood the mutual attraction because a friend of hers came to the root beer stand one evening to talk to me.

She said, "Mildred likes you, and would like to go out with you, but her father said she can't go out with a Mexican. She asked me to break it to you in a nice way."

I became withdrawn during my high school years, not caring to discuss my insecurities with anyone; my self-esteem plummeted. I could not carry on a lucid conversation with anyone other than family members and close friends. I was an outsider in two cultures.

With my *güero* friends I might say, "*Wuthering Heights* is showing at the Tivoli uptown. Wanna go?"

In the barrio it would be, "I have *ganas* to see *Viva Villa* at the Pearl."

Before, during, and after the Tivoli show we were typical American teenagers, passing the time as *güero* teenagers did in other Ohio towns. In the barrio our activities were affected by various Mexican cultural traditions and habits, one of which was a restriction on associating too closely with Chicanas our age unless supervised by an adult sister, aunt, or older female friend of the family.

The barrio, exercising its inexorable pull, never left me while I mixed with my *güero* friends. If it was a windy night, the gusts echoing eerily along the Black River brought back memories of *La Llorona*, "The Wailing Lady," whose spirit was destined to mourn forever the drowning of her children. My Chicano friends and I had outgrown the myth, but there were Mexicans who believed in the tragedy as fact, as true as their family stories, passed down through generations, of an ancestor who buried gold treasures in a location known only to witches or to an adversary who stole the gold. To them it was not merely a suspension of disbelief, nor the magical realism of their *Macondo* villages. Although I did not empathize with this view, my outright rejection of it would be an act of disloyalty to my heritage, or so I felt. I was compelled to demonstrate my pride in my Mexican descent. A *güero* stranger hearing my Midwestern English once asked if I was Spanish.

"No, I'm Mexican," I stated.

"But you can't be Mexican. You talk just like me," he said.

"No! I am Mexican!" I reiterated.

It was an unwitting paraphrase of the Chicano inside joke: "After you make a million dollars, you are no longer Mexican, you are Spanish."

And the listener's rejoinder: "Some Mexicans don't wait to make a million dollars. They become Spanish at the first opportunity."

Mixing with *güeros,* I was a Mexican. Living with Mexicans, I was an American. In high school I could not resolve these disparate pressures on my psyche. In my mind, I was a person without a nationality. It was a state of being that held me captive for years.

❈

In the spring of 1940 Mama arranged for Joe and me to work the summer months on the *betabel* with a Mexican family. We saw it as an opportunity to bring in more money than we could earn at summer jobs, if we could find them. The Zamora family rented a dilapidated house in Venice, a small crossroads village twenty miles directly west of Lorain. Drinking water came from a hand-pumped well; the toilet was a one-hole outhouse.

My brother and I shared an upstairs bedroom with three other young men Joe's age. I slept on the floor on a quilt sewn together by my grandmother. She asked me to sleep on the twin bed with Joe so that she would not have to wash the quilt so often. I refused. The thought of sharing a bed with anyone was completely unacceptable to me. I was incapable at that stage of my life of having any close physical contact with another person. My brother had the bed to himself. The others shared a double bed.

Señora Zamora cooked for her family and the five of us renting the upstairs bedroom. Early in the spring, she planted a garden of tomatoes, carrots, spinach, string beans, corn, peas, peppers, and lettuce. A general store a block away provided flour, rice, pinto beans, potatoes, beef, live chickens, and other staples. A charge account was maintained by the owner in a notebook, and was signed by the Zamoras after each purchase.

Señora Zamora prepared tortillas each morning and again in the early evening. The clapping sound of her hands as she made them accompanied her low humming of a bolero or a *corrido.* Breakfast was coffee, tortillas, and scrambled eggs. Our practiced fingers scooped up the eggs in small shovel-shaped pieces of tortilla. The noon meal consisted of tacos of refried beans mixed with pieces of bite-size chicken or beef and was delivered to the fields by Señor Zamora.

After cleaning up in the Lake Erie inlet that was practically in our back-yard, we devoured a *sopa*, a soup of stew-size pieces of beef or chicken, chunks of potatoes, carrots, celery, and corn on the cob. Side dishes were pinto beans, garbanzos, fried rice tinted a reddish color by a tomato sauce, a lettuce and tomato salad, and of course, tortillas and chile sauce. Like almost every mature Mexican woman, Señora Zamora was very experienced in preparation of meals; the time lapse from killing a chicken (by expertly twisting its neck) and plucking the feathers to the actual serving of the meal was short enough that she could take a break between meals to gather strength for the next assault on her time.

We worked the *betabel*, competing with migrants who had been pursu-ing it for years, and we could not keep up with them. The *betabel* had not changed in over twenty years—sharpened hoe blades, stooped positions, stinging blisters, aching backs, sidewise shuffling under a blazing sun, and primitive living conditions were still the sine qua non. It was a difficult ex-perience for a "city boy," but it helped prepare me for more trying challenges in the future, even as it flaunted the irony of Natividad's offspring revisiting the life that he thought was behind his family for good.

In the fall there were part-time jobs that paid well for a schoolboy. Setting pins in a bowling alley seven nights a week brought in ten to twelve dollars, which amounted to twenty-five to thirty percent of the take-home pay of a steel plant laborer. I worked the summer of 1942 as a laborer for the Nickel Plate Railroad, a passenger line running through the uptown area and serv-ing as part of the connecting link between Chicago and New York. We col-lected trash along the railroad right-of-way, unloaded boxcars, stacked metal parts in the warehouse, and kept the gandy dancers supplied with spikes and holding plates. It was my first real "grown up" job.

At age seventeen, I earned thirty-five dollars a week as a laborer in the steel mill. When the labor gang did a job in the Bessemer plant where my father worked, I spent the lunch breaks in monosyllabic talks with him and his co-workers. After quitting time, the men met at a cantina to drink a few beers and continue the lunchtime conversations, talking endlessly about life in Mexico and the *betabel*. I usually sat at the edge of the discussions, sipping a root beer and wondering how I could be so much a part of that culture and still not feel its attraction as powerfully as I felt the pull of the American Midwest.

In high school my social alienation continued, albeit on a reduced scale. I did not participate comfortably in conversations, and did not date. I remained an honor student and selected several college preparatory classes. I had no plan or desire to attend a college—it was almost unheard of in the early 1940s for a Chicano in Lorain to aspire to attend college. By 1941 only a handful had graduated from high school. I was confident that I could earn a high school diploma, but I considered it simply a step toward an eventual office job at the National Tube Company. I selected Algebra II, physics, and a foreign language only because I wanted to compete on their terms with students I viewed as being part of an elitist clan. My choice of German instead of Spanish as a foreign language was my naive way of trying to be different. The Spanish-language teacher was known among Chicanos as someone who refused to face the reality of the use of spoken Spanish in modern life. She insisted that "Castilian" Spanish was the proper pronunciation of the language and that spoken "Mexican" Spanish was the vulgate form. She was alleged to have said, "We will speak only Castilian Spanish in this class!"

The German-language teacher was outstanding. After four semesters, I learned to read and write the language as well as the second-generation immigrant students of German descent who spoke the language with their parents and wrote in German to their grandparents. I could converse in German haltingly by searching in my mental dictionary for the proper word or idiomatic expression. The teacher did not insist on a "high" or "low" pronunciation of certain words, and made no statement as to the "correct" use of the spoken word.

The absence of ambition in my plans for an education beyond high school was influenced by a custom among *la gente,* our people, that whenever a person of Mexican descent showed signs of trying to "move up" by, for example, enrollment in college, relocation from the barrio, or formal recognition of accomplishment by prominent *güeros,* that person was held up to ridicule for trying to be better than *la gente.* It is an oversimplification to refer to that reaction as envy. It was a trait ingrained in Mexicans generations earlier, and carried over the border more recently in the flow of migrant workers from Mexico.

❈ ❈ ❈

CHAPTER FIVE

World War II

On a Sunday afternoon on December 7, 1941, I was with a group of friends after the matinee at the Pearl Theater. As we walked down the street, we heard loud voices emanating from houses on both sides of the street. People came out of their houses, talking excitedly with their neighbors.

"Pearl Harbor? Where is that?"

"Hawaii."

"The Hawaiian Islands?"

"Yes!"

"Why?"

"Don't know. But you can be sure that we'll get even."

That "day of infamy" was to result in a major change in the lives of millions of Americans. As in the rest of the country, life in South Lorain changed suddenly as young men were drafted into the military services or enlisted out of patriotism brought on by the country's involvement in World War II. The loss of a large part of the labor pool and an increase in production vacancies as manufacturing emerged from the doldrums of the Great Depression created work opportunities for women and men under age eighteen. Mary and Jessie were employed as garment workers at a clothing factory. Josie continued her high school studies. Joe was not able to get a job because of his epilepsy.

Work at the clothing factory was typical of garment industry jobs, repetitive and unimaginative, designed for lowly paid, semiskilled workers. It provided a living if the worker was not the only breadwinner in the family. It also filled a need among the mostly Mexican American workforce for a gathering place to discuss matters of consequence to their families and to enjoy gossip, a necessary ingredient in the makeup of the Mexican American community.

As the war continued into and through 1942, the country experienced shortages of certain foods, clothing, and other consumer goods produced by industries now dedicated to war production. The acquisition of material goods had never been a high priority effort in our family, and now, with little opportunity to spend discretionary income, our financial standing improved, although it was still below what today would be called the poverty line. The specter of war hung over our everyday thoughts and actions. It could not be avoided. It was everywhere, in the news, in our conversations, in the transportation difficulties resulting from gasoline rationing, and in high school activities that emphasized preparation of male seniors for entry into military service. It was brought home painfully whenever a soldier from South Lorain was reportedly killed in action.

Mary continually encouraged Josie to remain in school, and Josie graduated from high school in June 1943, a distinction rarely achieved by Mexican Americans at that time. She was the first to do so in our family. She had overcome the difficulty of faithfully attending classes among jostling, exuberant classmates who were at times not very tolerant of her physical disabilities. After graduation, Josie joined her sisters in the clothing factory, slowly walking the two blocks to and from Pearl Avenue. Ohio winters, with their heavy snowfalls and slippery sidewalks, created nightmares for her.

I was in the first semester of my senior year in early 1943, and along with my classmates and our respective families, I grew more and more apprehensive of an uncertain future after graduation.

In May 1943 I told my sisters and grandmother, "I have been reading a lot about Guadalcanal Island in the Pacific Ocean, and how the First and Second Marine Divisions have beaten the odds to defeat the Japanese for control of the island. I want to join the Marines."

Mary said, "Are you crazy? You're only seventeen years old and you have to finish high school. You graduate next January. You can wait until you turn eighteen and get your draft notice, or sign up for the navy's V-12 program, as you told me a couple of months ago."

Grandmother, Josie, and Jessie nodded in agreement.

I said, "I can't wait for all of that. My friends are enlisting in the army or navy or are being drafted right now. I can't imagine spending the next eight months here without any of the guys to pal around with. As for the V-12 program, the navy requires two years of college studies before a commission can be awarded. They will provide the college level courses, but heck, the war will probably be over by the time I'm eligible for the commission."

I took the enlistment papers to my father and said, "I want to enlist in the Marines, but you have to sign these papers because I'm not eighteen years old yet."

He asked, "Are you sure you want to join the Marines?"

I said, "Yes."

He signed the papers, and said, "I want to go with you to the train station when they tell you to report for basic training."

I was dumbfounded. I never expected him to say anything like that. Our relations had been very formal since he placed us in the orphanage. There had been no expressions of affection, no embraces, no queries by me, and no fatherly advice by him.

I passed the physical exam, took the oath of service, and was assigned June 21, 1943, as the date to report to the Marine enlistment office in Cleveland for transportation to the recruit depot at Parris Island, South Carolina.

When I told Mary about our father's intention to go to Cleveland with me, she said, "Good. I'm also going with you. We can all go on the same bus. By the way, I've told my friends that you are joining the Marines, and I am very proud of you."

On reporting day, Mary and I got on the bus at Vine Avenue with the understanding that our father would board at the next stop. As the bus approached Pearl Avenue, it did not slow down. A passenger shouted, "Hey, driver, there are people waiting to be picked up at that stop."

He shouted back, "Another bus is right behind us. We always run two buses at this hour."

As we passed Pearl Avenue, we saw the questioning look on our father's face, his arms extended, the palms facing up and his mouth voicing, "What's going on?"

The buses arrived in Cleveland, and we walked together to the Marine enlistment office. The marine sergeant told me, "OK, I've checked you in. Report to the train station by 5:00 P.M. You are now in the Marine Corps, and you had better be on time."

As we left the building, I said, "I have five hours to kill. If you want to see me off at the train station, we might as well catch a movie, or just hang around the stores on Euclid Avenue and the Terminal Tower."

We ate lunch at a cafeteria and agreed to watch a movie to pass the time. The film featured Tyrone Power playing the part of a submarine officer. The cartoon was a Tom and Jerry episode in which the cat and mouse challenged each other by performing a piano recital, Franz Liszt's Hungarian Rhapsody.

We arrived at the train station before 5:00 P.M. I checked my name off the list of recruits and we milled around in the station with several hundred other people, awaiting the booming voice of a marine sergeant. The three of us did not carry on much of a conversation. Mary and I could not conduct with our father the intimate discussions that family members normally associate with an event like the departure of another family member for an unknown length of time and an uncertain future.

Finally, the marine sergeant called out, "Recruits! Board the train!"

I was surprised to see my father turn and wipe away a tear. I embraced my sister and father and climbed aboard with excited anticipation of new adventures. For over fifty years, each time I hear the Liszt piano piece, I clearly recall those last few hours of my departure for Marine Corps basic training.

❋

Marine boot camp was everything that has ever been written, spoken, or filmed about it. On a daily basis it left one alternately depressed and elevated, humbled and proud, enervated and strengthened. But in the end it accomplished what it was designed to do: instill in a diverse group of men a strong sense of unity, and in the individual a confidence that he can overcome almost any obstacle that threatens to prevent him from reaching his goal.

The B&O Railroad passenger cars in which we left Cleveland for Parris Island, South Carolina, were packed with seated civilians and Marine recruits standing, squatting, or sitting on suitcases and bags in the aisles. Women and children accepted seats offered by men courteously observing that custom. It was a feat for a male to elbow and push his way through the crowded aisles to the toilet or open platform for a smoke or a breath of fresh air.

When a woman or child needed to use the restroom, space opened up quickly, and they moved to the head of the line, accompanied by shouts, "Lady with baby coming through!"

Three races were represented among the passengers, but when the train stopped in Washington, the blacks disappeared, or so it seemed. I did not realize that they were in a separate car until the next morning when we arrived at Beaufort, South Carolina, and they poured out of the rearmost car, obviously more tightly packed than ours. It was my first observation of legal racial segregation, an unsettling moment for a young idealist. It was merely the beginning of an increased exposure to racial incidents that I soon learned existed in everyday life in many parts of the country, mostly in the South.

Over the next few months the bigotry among some recruits and noncommissioned officers (many of whom I respected for being "a few good men") continued to bother me, even as I realized that they were probably merely echoing words and phrases that they had grown up with, much as I had adopted the "most-*güeros*-hate-Mexicans" syndrome. The Marine Corps was not racially integrated during World War II; there were no blacks in the Parris Island boot camp, but that did not stop the derogatory statements about their race.

It was especially galling to hear the lies and distortions about Jews and their forebears. The Jews in the platoon remained silent and appeared to reach into themselves for the quiet strength to overcome the insults. I had known only one Jew my age in Lorain, and I admired his courage in facing up to the verbal assaults of others. We became friends and were not familiar with each other's religious beliefs and practices. It was not because we consciously avoided discussing them. He was a Jew and I was a Catholic—there was nothing more to talk about on that subject. It was the same situation concerning my friendship with Dick, whom I knew to be a Protestant only because I would see him and his parents going to their church on Sundays. Again, we did not discuss our respective religions.

As we stepped off the train at the Beaufort station, marine sergeants met us with shouts that were to become a habit over the next eight weeks: "All recruits, over here! Line up! Move it! Move it!"

After an attendance check and assignment by name to forty-man platoons, the bellowing continued: "Into the buses. Move!"

We rode to Parris Island, the Marine Corps recruit depot.

The sergeants continued their ear-busting yells. "Out of the buses! Into the barbershop! Move! Move!"

The haircuts took about five minutes, the electric razors leaving a quarter-inch stubble and no sideburns. The next stop was the shower and dispensary where we stripped, placed our clothes in marked bags, and walked slowly through a continuous overhead shower, scrubbing vigorously with a bar of harsh soap and completing the cleansing process by stepping through an oblong pan filled with athlete's foot antiseptic. Our civilian clothes were taken from us and we were given large canvas "seabags." We filed through a quartermaster supply warehouse and filled the bags with government-issued undershorts, T-shirts, socks, boots, dungarees, canvas belt, and pith helmet. We lined up in shorts for a medical exam: stethoscope chest examination, the traditional "skin it back and milk it" gonorrhea drip test, then the "turn your head and cough" hernia check.

A few minutes later, we double timed to the barracks area as a drill instructor (DI) shouted, "Move!"

After the DI assigned us bunks, bedding, and foot lockers, we were instructed on the method of making the beds with "hospital-corners" and a blanket tension that forced a coin to bounce a few inches after being dropped on the tightened surface. We stored our gear in the footlocker exactly as shown on a diagram.

A DI said, "Pay attention, boots! You have just learned some of the basic things of life in the Marine Corps. You will not deviate one iota from what you have been instructed. Not one iota. You will follow orders exactly as they are given. No deviations! Now move out for close order drill."

The next few weeks we followed a grueling schedule of close order drill, marching up and down the parade field for hours at a time under a blazing summer sun. We performed the Manual of Arms until our movements with the M-1 rifle were so thoroughly synchronized that the slightest misstep or rifle fumble by an individual elicited not only a roar from the DI but also a subdued hiss by prideful platoon mates.

I became a "chowhound," one who frequently goes back for second helpings during meals. Something was driving my body to make up for the missing energy equivalents of earlier meals. As a teenager, I played well for the first half of basketball games and the first two games of a bowling match. As the game continued, my play became increasingly erratic by the time the game ended. In the Marine Corps, I played many pick-up games and a few competitive matches against other units and was strong throughout the game. The same situation applied in rigorous training exercises—I was in excellent shape at the end of the session, and after a shower and a good meal I was ready for more strenuous undertakings.

I had a bad childhood habit of eating hurriedly in order to stop the chant outside our house: "Hey Frank, come on, buddy. We're late for the game." My participation in these outings caused me to miss noon meals at home, and at times an evening meal. These eating habits did not contribute to an orderly growth and development pattern.

At Parris Island we took various aptitude tests, progressively reducing our selective group to about eight persons. Men with college exposure were informed that, after boot camp, they would be given advanced training in a specialty to be announced after more tests. Four of the tallest men with high school diplomas were assigned as platoon squad leaders.

The DI took me aside and said, "You are an anomaly—good test results, not a high school graduate, and too short to be considered for a leadership position. You will probably be assigned to some technical school instead of an infantry unit."

I was impressed with the evaluation and dedicated myself to being a good marine. I gained weight, grew an inch, and, except for challenges in which height and physical strength were premiums, was consistently near the top in competitive events. Those exercises that required stamina, endurance, or application of lessons learned were decisively in my favor.

I once received a DI comment, "Good going, Mendez. You're the first to arrive."

This occurred after a forced march of several miles, carrying rifles and full gear and applying an out-of-cadence step close to a full trot in order to be at a map location in no more than an unbelievably short time. Several men passed out or had to drop out because of sudden medical shortcomings—it was not unusual for men to faint on the parade ground during extended close order drill under a broiling sun. When it happened, the DIs would yell, "Leave him alone. Step over him. The corpsmen (medics) will handle it. Continue the march!"

There were many other incidents that left us with mixed feelings about our drill instructors. They were either sadists or dedicated professionals trying hard to turn out marines who would function well under combat conditions.

One night at a 10:00 P.M. "lights out," a boot whispered to his dozing neighbor, "I didn't make the chow line. What did you have for supper?"

The irritated bunkmate snapped, "Alligator ass."

A light chuckle in the darkness, and a stronger whisper added, "It was appetizing alligator ass!"

More chuckles, then another voice added, "It was really appetizing alligator ass à la Alabama."

Full laughter, and still another voice said, "No, no! It was fricasseed frog farts from Flor—."

Suddenly, the overhead lights came "ON" and the alliteration went "OFF." There stood a glowering DI.

He shouted, "It looks like you boots are not tired enough to fall asleep. Well, I'll take care of that. Move out in five minutes with rifles and full gear!"

Outside the barracks, he intoned, "Pla'TOON! Ten' SHUN! Port ARMS! Right FACE! Forward MARCH! DOUBLE TIME!"

For the next thirty minutes, we ran around the parade field perimeter over and over again, until finally, he said, "Pla'TOON! HALT! Left FACE! Order ARMS! FALL OUT! And I don't want to hear a word out of you until 0500 hours tomorrow."

There was no sound after 10:00 P.M. thereafter (except for some heavy snoring).

Toward the end of the eight-week basic training cycle the platoon was functioning well, meeting all objectives in exemplary fashion. I was actually enjoying boot camp, but I also looked forward to the next phase of my Marine Corps experience—graduation and a new assignment. Most of us expected to be assigned to combat units as replacements for troop losses and personnel rotating back to the United States to train and form new units.

I was assigned to the Artillery Fire Direction School at Camp Lejeune, North Carolina, where students learned to set and adjust azimuth and elevation for emplaced artillery pieces using tarage tables, slide rules, and plotting boards amid radio messages with forward observers and gun crew chiefs. After several weeks training, I was assigned to a newly established unit, the 17th Artillery Battalion. Instead of being incorporated into the Fire Direction Section, I was placed in the Perimeter Defense Squad, which consisted of eight machine gunners and a squad leader responsible for protecting the four 155mm guns and crews of "B" Battery by preparing and manning the machine gun positions that covered the front and flanks of the emplaced Long Toms.

Three months later, the battalion shipped out to San Diego, California, by railroad, where we boarded a troop transport containing our weapons and equipment. After eight days at sea, the ship sailed into Pearl Harbor, passing the battleships destroyed on December 7, 1941. Their rusting superstructures showed above water with oil slicks still swirling about the steel skeletons.

Just before our ship pulled into the harbor, hundreds of us had been chattering on deck in anticipation of viewing the site of probably the most historic incident in our lifetime. As we approached the first signs of the damage, conversations on deck suddenly stopped. They did not resume until the transport started its docking routine at one of the innermost piers. In later conversations it was generally agreed that the terrible scene of rusting battleship remnants, and all it implied, was an eye-opening alert of what lay ahead for American military forces in the Asiatic-Pacific theater of operations.

For me, it was a painful remembrance of the loss of two of my closest friends from our early childhood in South Lorain. Joe Weigl and Gene Basilone were aboard the USS *Liscome Bay* in November 1943 when it was torpedoed and sunk by a Japanese submarine in the Gilbert Islands during the amphibious invasion of Tarawa by the Second Marine Division. By way of coincidence, several months later I was attached to the 105mm artillery regiment of the Second Marine Division after it completed the Tarawa operation and was pulled back to the "Big Island" of Hawaii. It established Camp Tarawa there as a training base for upcoming amphibious operations.

When we disembarked at Pearl Harbor, we learned that the 17th Artillery Battalion was assigned to the Fifth Amphibious Corps Artillery, Fleet Marine Force. Our mission was to provide long-range artillery support to Marine infantry units during an amphibious operation. This meant that we could not participate in the small island invasions underway and being planned because our 155mm guns would overshoot Japanese fortifications. On checking a map of the Pacific area, I noticed that the only feasible use of our unit would be for an invasion of the main islands of Japan itself. Nevertheless, we prepared for any assignment that higher authority might order. It is a Marine Corps creed that all marines are capable of fighting as infantrymen, regardless of their specialized training or current assignment.

The battalion spent a week at the Pearl Harbor transient-unit tent city awaiting an order to relocate. When it came, we shipped out on an inter-island steamer to the island of Kauai where we helped the navy's Construction Battalion build our marine tent camp on a farm between the towns of Kapaa and Lihue. We trained there, firing inert ammunition at anchored targets in the ocean, conducting infantry exercises, and generally keeping in shape for any eventuality.

Several months later I was placed on orders to take part in a 105mm howitzer artillery firing exercise on the island of Hawaii. I flew in a C-47 cargo plane from Barking Sands Army Air Corps Base to the Naval Air Station at Hilo, Hawaii, along with a dozen other artillery troops who were reporting for temporary duty with the Second Marine Division. We trained at Camp Tarawa with the division's 105mm artillery regiment that was conducting the exercise in preparation for its next combat operation. The training was in fire direction center operations; my permanent unit did not inform me why I was selected for a task in which I had no recent experience. It really did not bother me. I was glad to be associated with the Second Marine Division in any capacity. I wanted to be with the best, and it was the Second Marine Division's accomplishments at Guadalcanal that had spurred me on to enlisting in the Marine Corps.

Camp Tarawa was located near the small town of Kamuela on the huge Parker cattle ranch. Its size easily accommodated a twenty-thousand-man marine division with a tent city, a maneuver area for its infantry regiments, and a firing range for the artillery regiment—all the while operating a ranch whose fresh beef product was consumed by a clientele consisting of Hawaiian Islands civilians and thousands of military personnel in the Asiatic-Pacific theater.

The camp was reached from Hilo by military vehicle on a temporary road cut by military engineers over a saddle between the extinct Mauna Kea and the active Mauna Loa volcanoes. There was also a paved highway that ran from Hilo to Kamuela along the coast, passing picturesque pineapple and sugar cane plantations and yielding breathtaking views of flowering bougainvillea and hibiscus bushes and many varieties of palm trees on terrain rising gradually to the slopes of the Mauna Kea. Plantation residents and day workers were the primary users of the highway; light military vehicles also used the paved road, even though it took much longer to get to Kamuela over its winding turns.

As the field exercise progressed, several of us on temporary duty asked the first sergeant if we could be permanently assigned to the Second Marine Division.

The "top sergeant" said, "You men have been identified to form a pool of available replacements in various specialties. After you get back to your unit, you could be levied to fill, by the most rapid means possible, the combat losses of another unit whose effectiveness has been compromised by unexpected casualties. You kids want to be heroes. You've got to get that idea out of your head. I don't want heroes in my unit. I want men who, in combat, will concentrate on the mission, look out for their buddies, and follow my orders no matter how piddling they might seem. I don't want to see some asshole making a Hollywood charge at a machine gun nest when we are pinned down. I want to figure out how to take it without losing any of my troops. You need to get back to your units and apply the lessons you've learned from those of us who have been under fire."

His gunnery sergeant language, in all its sincerity, was appropriate to the situation. It was only much later that I realized how well he had captured the thoughts of another leader of many centuries past. He did not want to have

to deliver a Prince Hal epitaph over a lifeless Hotspur who had vowed to
seek glory in a coming battle:

> By heaven, methinks it were an easy leap,
> To pluck bright honour from the pale-faced moon,
> Or dive into the bottom of the deep,
> Where fathom-line could never touch the ground,
> And pluck up drowned honour by the locks.

The "top's" concern about the unbridled drives of eighteen-year-old Marines did not impress me that I was one who needed to be restrained from
taking foolhardy risks. I acknowledged that I carried an obligation to "pay
my dues" by seeking combat experience but not at the cost of exposing my
buddies to additional enemy fire. I traced the retention of this undisclosed
guilt to my not being assigned to an infantry unit after boot camp. It led to
my conclusion that our battalion had evolved to a state described by John
Milton, "They also serve who only stand and wait." Those beautiful, lasting,
self-appraising words of a genius gave me small comfort when I thought of
Joe Weigl, Gene Basilone, and others who had put their lives on the line for
our community and our nation.

The two-week training session and field exercise ended; we flew back to
Kauai and returned to our respective units. Within a month the Second Ma-
rine Division left Camp Tarawa and launched an amphibious invasion of the
Marianas Islands.

Word-of-mouth and after-action reports of the Saipan Island operation
fulfilled the first sergeant's augury. The Japanese defenders were pushed to a
peninsular area that ended at an escarpment overlooking the ocean. Many
hurled themselves off the precipice, perishing on the wave-washed rocks hundreds of feet below. Their leaders organized an infamous, suicidal "Banzai"
charge. Battalions of enemy soldiers, screaming hideously, raced toward the
advancing Marine infantry companies, the Japanese officers brandishing
swords and firing pistols, their subordinates firing rifles or holding grenades
with a pulled pin.

Hundreds of Japanese and dozens of marines died as the chargers over-
ran the line and continued to the rear, sweeping by the Marine second line
in diminishing numbers and finally arriving at the rear echelon where hast-
ily assembled units and artillery perimeter defense machine guns in enfilade
defended the emplaced 105mm howitzers, awaiting the remaining elements

of enemy troops. The gun crews set the fuses for super-quick arming and fired round after round at zero degrees elevation into the crazed chargers dozens of yards in front of the howitzers. Few Japanese survived the withering Marine fire; the banzai charge ended there.

I never heard of the first sergeant's fate in that battle.

The Fifth Marine Division replaced the Second Marine Division at Camp Tarawa, and after a few months of organizing and training, left in January 1945 for its initial combat operation, the amphibious assault on Iwo Jima. Again we remained behind because our 155mm guns had too long a range for islands the size of Iwo Jima.

In January 1945 the 17th Artillery Battalion left Kauai for Camp Tarawa where we were able to conduct long-range firing exercises at ground targets simulating enemy positions. We left Hawaii for Guam in March 1945 after the Third Marine Division reclaimed the island. We remained on Guam two months after hostilities ended in August 1945 and returned to the continental United States, arriving at San Diego on November 10, 1945. A few days later, the 17th Artillery Battalion was disestablished at Camp Pendleton, California. We received individual travel orders for Marine Corps destinations as close as possible to our respective homes, awaiting honorable discharges, or new assignments for those who chose to remain in the Marine Corps.

❋

On the long train ride from San Diego to Cleveland, I passed the hours thinking back on the last two and one-half years; several incidents are inscribed indelibly in my memory. Three close friends with whom I spent hours almost every day over a ten-year period were not returning to Lorain. Joe Weigl, Gene Basilone, and Frank Dominguez were part of our "Vine Avenue Gang." On reading letters reporting that they had been killed in action, I felt that I had lost three brothers.

"Pancho" Dominguez left a void that was never to be filled; he and I would never assemble another team to compete in softball, bowling, or table tennis leagues. He was a superbly coordinated athlete who quickly became the star of every team he joined. He was the pitcher and leading hitter of our softball team, the bowler with the highest average in the city-wide Class C Men's League, and the perennial winner of the YMCA table tennis tournament (all between the ages of fifteen to eighteen). He was killed in action in Europe during the Battle of the Bulge.

It slowly dawned on me that the past and the future were permanently divorced—it was not possible to re-create the life we left behind after entering the military service. Any thoughts I had had of picking up and continuing the barrio life I had led were erased by the time the train pulled into the Cleveland railroad station. I knew that the present had to serve as a transition between the irreplaceable past and the uncertain future.

I did not know what I would do after the war ended. While still on Guam, I was notified by Lorain High School administrators that a recent change in Ohio statutes permitted award of a high school diploma to veterans who had completed two semesters of State of Ohio civics courses and seven semesters of high school English studies. I had fulfilled both requirements prior to enlisting in the Marine Corps; I received the diploma in absentia. I also learned that Congress had passed the GI Bill, which provided a veteran full college tuition, fees, and course materials if he enrolled in a college whose costs were comparable to those of a state university. It also gave the veteran seventy-five dollars a month for living expenses, if he carried a full schedule of classes.

I arrived in Lorain in December 1945 to start a thirty-day furlough granted to all military personnel returning from overseas deployment. After a two-year separation from my family, it was a euphoric moment to join them again. We reinforced the bond that had held us together through near disasters and other trying situations. The joy we shared during the Christmas holidays was dampened somewhat by the approaching end of my furlough and the necessity to make a decision that would result in a major change in my life. I had to decide by January 31, 1946, whether to continue to serve in the Marine Corps or to request a discharge.

I reported to my next assignment at the Marine barracks at Bainbridge Naval Station in Maryland after the furlough ended. I decided to leave the United States Marine Corps, and was issued an honorable discharge on February 1, 1946.

My decision to leave the Marine Corps was not easy. The experience imbued me with qualities that helped me later in life, giving me a confidence to undertake tough actions with little fear of failure. I enjoyed the close friendships, the camaraderie, and the challenges, as represented in the Agincourt spirit, "We few, we happy few, we band of brothers."

My promotion to corporal less than two years after enlisting, despite being the youngest member of my squad, confirmed the strength of my attachment—my squad mates responded positively to the promotion. I never

Corp. Frank S. Mendez, U.S. Marine Corps, January 1946. *Author's collection.*

had reason to suspect lack of support, jealousy, or racial bias. They were outstanding; we got the job done. I left the Marine Corps with a poignancy that bordered on homesickness. But life as a marine had also taught me to move on after a mission is accomplished.

CHAPTER SIX

❈ ❈ ❈

Civilian Life

Chicano veterans were no different from other men in needing time to relax and adjust to civilian life after returning to our hometowns. In Lorain, the most popular form of relaxation was drinking beer at a cantina while telling war stories that grew in humor or battle description as the evening advanced. As the drinking progressed, our language regressed to repetition of prewar jokes and incidents in "Spanglish," and to Mexican songs we sang years ago. Over and over we repeated "*El Hijo Desobediente*," a ballad about a disobedient son who threatens to harm his father for challenging his manhood by trying to keep him from fighting another macho.

The cantina was our postwar "clubhouse." We drank beer as we planned various projects, none of them very well thought out. A sudden decision to enter a county basketball or table tennis tournament always resulted in our team being eliminated in the first or second round. We joked about the losses and washed down our defeats with a few more beers. A Friday night decision to attend a Chicano dance in Cleveland on Saturday night usually ended up with only two or three of us going to the dance and returning shortly after with no "conquests" to brag about. Several projects ended stillborn.

After the standard three-beer relaxer one night, Louie announced, "I promised my *güera* that we would sing the *Mañanitas* tomorrow on her birthday."

"Great idea," said Carlos. "Where you gonna get the *cantantes?*"

"*Aquí*, right here," said Louie. "We can sing it."

"*Menso*, dummy. We don't know the words," said Carlos.

Louie said, "*Es* easy. It starts out, '*Esta es la Mañanita.*'"

"No, *cabrón,*" I said. "It's, '*Estas son las Mañanitas.*' I don't know the rest of the song."

"Neither do I," said Louie. "Does anyone know the rest of the song?"

"No. Me *no sabe, tonto,* and it's a lousy idea anyway," said Carlos. "Gimme another beer."

Over the next few months, the drinking and singing faded away as we took on more responsible pursuits. Individually, we had already begun to lose the use of barrio Spanglish and the accompanying accent. Its demise was initiated during the war by daily conversations with *güero* buddies, and accelerated after the war by an increased rate of intermarriage with *güeras* and an expansion of the invisible barrio border into areas of Lorain where neighbors did not speak Spanish.

Veterans throughout the country began to put their lives together again. We returned to prewar jobs, resumed high school or college studies, married, bought a house, or started a family, many engaging in several of these at once. I decided to enroll in college, but I needed to build up my academic background by taking the second semester high school courses I missed when I enlisted in my senior year. School administrators cooperated by scheduling my subjects for the first four class hours and excusing me from all other activities.

I claimed my old laborer job at the National Tube Company (a legal right of returning veterans), requesting the 3:00 P.M. to 11:00 P.M. shift. It was an unusual job, one to which only new employees were assigned and rotated out of in a few months. I preferred the job because of the frequent rest breaks during which I did my homework or caught up on my reading. The work was in the rolling mills, directly below huge metal rollers on which red-hot blooms of alloyed steel two-feet square and eight-feet long were rolled into and squeezed between powerful dies that formed them into bars and flat strips that were then rolled into the pipe mills for further processing into tubing and pipe.

As the blooms moved on the rollers, pieces of red-hot scale the size of a slice of toast peeled off, falling between the rollers onto a metal V-shaped roof, inverted to allow the scale to slide down its slopes. The pieces dropped off the roof into gutter-shaped troughs on each side of a concrete walkway on which we worked wearing heavy boots, padded trousers, wire-mesh gloves, and an asbestos hood that covered the head and shoulders down to the waist.

The scale built up in the troughs. We shoveled it into wheelbarrows, taking care to remain as close as possible to the center of the walkway to minimize risks of being hit by the falling red hot scale. An occasional piece bounced out of the trough, singeing boots or trousers.

After filling the wheelbarrow, we pushed it down the walkway, upended it into a huge dumpster-like bucket, raised the container by electric hoist, and emptied it into a dump truck outside the mill. We were required to take twenty-minute breaks each hour to limit our exposure to the hazardous operation. No one in our crew suffered any apparent health problems in the six months I worked there.

❋

In early September 1946 I accompanied my father on a three-week trip to Mexico City and his hometown. He had not visited Zirosto since his hurried departure three decades earlier. On our arrival at the Los Reyes train station, a cousin met us and led us on horseback on the mountain trail that still served as the community's link to the outside world. We could see the smoke flume of the Paricutín volcano from a distance. The volcanic cone had formed to a height of several hundred feet; it still ejected large rocks while rivulets of molten lava flowed from its sides. The only presence in the Paricutín town was the church tower projecting above the hardened lava field. Volcanic ash covered the countryside all the way to Zirosto and its surrounding hills.

Some of my first cousins whose parents had moved to Mexico City were doing well economically and academically. Those remaining behind in Ziros-to, according to my father, were living the simple life that he had lived; he pointed out that the walls of his family's house were no longer adobe, but wood slats, and the floor was made of mortise-and-tenon planks of wood. Although my cousins, uncles, and aunts were strangers, I was perfectly at home with them, conversing easily in Spanish without the subconscious anxiety I sometimes experienced in Lorain when talking to *güero* strangers. It fostered my thoughts of the possibility of a career in a Latin American country.

The trip back to Ohio was therapeutic for us in the sense that, for the first time in our lives, my father and I had the opportunity to push aside the wall between us that had deflected previous attempts by either of us to reach out to the other with personal comments or questions. The barrier was not breached on the way to Mexico, undoubtedly because we needed a more extended pe-riod of time to overcome the unease of spending twenty-four hours a day in each other's presence.

Only twice in more than ten years had we spent more than two hours to-gether. I ran into him one day at the bowling alley where I worked setting pins,

Frank and Natividad Mendez in Mexico City, September 1946. *Author's collection.*

and he invited me to join him in the fish-fry special. The food was delicious. I
had not eaten in a restaurant before, or had a dinner with such a variety of side
dishes. Another time a friend and I were hitchhiking to the Lake Erie beaches
when my father and a boarding house acquaintance drove up and offered us a
lift. At the beach, we spent an hour or so in our two separate groups. My buddy
and I then continued our outing in other directions.

The two incidents could just as easily have taken place with a distant uncle or an adult friend of the family, for all the father-son impression they made on me. More descriptive of our actual relationship was a situation involving a dental bill. At age sixteen, on my own initiative, I had gone to a dentist for major work that involved cleaning a green growth off teeth that I never brushed and filling large cavities in several teeth that were at least ten percent rotten. The secretary routinely asked me for my father's name and address, and I, without realizing why she wanted it, gave it to her. Several weeks later, I went to see him to pick up the biweekly support stipend.

He handed me a dental bill for sixteen dollars and asked, "What's this all about?"

I answered, "Oh, you weren't supposed to get that. I'll take care of it."

He gave me the biweekly amount. I thanked him and we parted with no further discussion. He did not comment on the condition of my teeth. I paid the bill with my earnings from the pin-setting job. It had not occurred to me before or after the dental work that he should pay the bill.

I found him to be a loner, a personality type not uncommon among men. In my teenage years, and more than a few times as an adult, I experienced similar feelings, withdrawing from close contact with other persons, preferring to spend hours by myself, reading or simply observing the neighborhood, the woods, and the open fields. Over the next few years we drew gradually into something that, because of my age, I would characterize as more of a brother-brother than a father-son relationship. He married again after twenty years as a widower and had a son who is twenty-four years my junior; they appeared to be a happy family. My sisters and I drew closer to him and his new family, pleased to know that he would be accompanied by a wife and son who would be present when he needed them.

He was an exemplary employee who worked hard at the only real job he ever held—second man, and ultimately straw boss of a Bessemer process crew. His work was demanding and hazardous. At least once he suffered extensive second-degree burns from molten steel that spurted inadvertently from the Bessemer converter; his injuries confined him on the National Tube Company's ward of Saint Joseph Hospital for several weeks.

"Nati" Mendez died at age sixty-two after a severe heart attack. He is buried in the same cemetery as my mother and brother. His second wife moved to California with my half-brother shortly thereafter.

❊ ❊ ❊

CHAPTER SEVEN

Searching for Respectability

I started classes at Bowling Green State University in Bowling Green, Ohio, in September 1946. The GI Bill covered all college costs and provided qualified veterans with seventy-five dollars a month for living expenses. I had no financial problems, given my frugal lifestyle. With the fifteen to twenty dollars a month I earned from part-time jobs in the maintenance department, I was able to contribute a few dollars a month to help my sisters care for our grandmother and brother. I had done so earlier with my Marine Corps and civilian job pay. It was a cultural obligation routinely assumed by grown barrio children of families with limited means.

I enjoyed my studies, making the dean's list each semester. Being on the honors list gave me several privileges, one of which was permission to take two extra classes each semester. Another benefit was the right to cut classes without penalty (exception: no makeups permitted on tests or exams), a privilege I exercised on classes I found boring or sometimes mistakenly thought were irrelevant. My goal was not necessarily to graduate with honors, but to get started on a career as soon as possible. I compensated easily for the lower grades I received in the classes I cut by maintaining a 4.0 grade point average in my major courses and other subjects I really enjoyed.

By the end of my sophomore year, I had earned extra credit hours by carrying greater semester and summer session loads (including an intensive postsummer session). Additionally, veterans were granted credit hours for college equivalent military service; I qualified for the permissible maximum. My adviser informed me that if I continued carrying extra loads, which he did not recommend, I would meet minimum requirements for major, minor, and total credit hours and could graduate early with a degree in mathematics.

Obviously, compressing the programmed time of the usual four-year college degree deprives a student of many extracurricular influences and associations that are an important part of the total college experience. Returning veterans in 1946 formed a large percentage of the student body. We brought with us a skeptical view of participation in spirited rallies for intercollegiate athletic contests, fraternity rushes, spontaneous pranks (panty raids), some formal social events, and all rah-rah school spirit boosters. I was one of the spoilsports, even while sympathizing with nonveteran freshman who were aware of our dampening influence on their social expectations. Within a couple of years our percentage decreased and our influence diminished. The pendulum completed its cycle, and the nonveterans were able to live fully the college life they had anticipated as high school seniors.

Although I rarely dated on campus or in Lorain, I was not antisocial. I was single-mindedly in pursuit of academic knowledge and career preparation, which in my mind left little time for social activities. I had tempered my sensitivity to racist comments or incidents by men, thanks in great part to the hardening experience of Marine Corps life. But I retained a subdued wariness toward getting too close to *güeras,* still wanting to interpret a date refusal as a racial putdown.

At a social event for foreign students in February 1948, I met Leticia Carles Guardia, a first-year student from Panama. Her beauty, her long, wavy, auburn hair, and the ease with which she mixed with group after group caught my attention immediately. We were engaged by the time she graduated.

During the period between the end of summer classes and the start of the fall semester, some students remaining in the university area worked at the Heinz catsup factory. We took jobs in the tomato processing line, unloading crates of farm-picked tomatoes, culling out the bad ones, and spray washing the good tomatoes on the conveyor belt.

Migrant farm workers picked the vegetables in the nearby fields. They lived under conditions that my family had experienced in Iowa in 1925 and in northern Ohio in 1940. From time to time, Lety and I chatted with a few who worked in the plant cafeteria.

One Sunday morning, as Lety and I left the Catholic church after mass, a Mexican family approached us, the mother carrying a six-month-old baby.

The father said, "*Buenos días.* We are migrant farm workers, and we want you to baptize our baby. Will you be his godparents?"

I said, *"Buenos dias.* I don't know how we can become secondary parents to a child. We are geographical transients, and so are you. We will not be able to attend to his religious obligations."

He replied, *"Está bien.* But we do not know any other people who can serve as godparents."

Lety stepped in and said, *"Bueno.* We will do it."

We drove out to their home to become familiar with the family and the child. The old unpainted farmhouse was practically falling apart; if it were within the city limits, it would probably have been condemned for occupancy. They had three other children, none of them more than ten years old, all of them playing in the dirt surrounding the shack. We did not enter the house. The smell in the air of urine and rancid pork stirred vague memories in me of our family's life in the early 1930s, living among newly arrived *betabeleros* and getting settled in housing not much better than that of the *betabel.*

On baptismal day, Lety and I took a white infant suit and blanket to their house. Lety washed the baby in a rudimentary kitchen sink outside the building, cleaning the encrusted dirt from his ears and nostrils with cotton swabs. We dressed him and took him to the church for the sacrament.

Two weeks later we went to visit them with canned goods and used children's clothing we had gathered from religious charities. The house was empty. We never saw them again. I do not remember my godson's name.

I graduated in June 1949 and was awarded a BGSU fellowship to work on a master's degree in mathematics. Two semesters and two summer sessions later I received the degree and learned that a national recession had severely limited job opportunities in every field in which a degree was required, or desired. I returned to Lorain and took a clerical job in the accounting office of the factory that produced the LORAIN mobile crane.

My brother Joe had shown no improvement in his medical condition; he continued to have epileptic seizures. The general practitioner who treated him indicated that his condition was incurable. In 1945 while I was overseas, Joe injured himself during a period of instability that had recurred increasingly after his grand mal seizures. City health officials recommended that he be placed in the state hospital for epileptics at Gallipolis on the Ohio River, approximately 175 miles away, where he could receive special treatment. It was a difficult decision for my grandmother and sisters; after a few days they reluctantly agreed, and Joe was taken to Gallipolis by the state of Ohio. Grandmother suffered the apparent loss of her grandson and close companion in silence.

Joe and Mary Mendez at the Ohio Hospital for Epileptics, Gallipolis, Ohio, in the late 1940s. *Mendez family archives.*

She was really too frail to travel, but she summoned the strength to go with Mary by bus across the state to visit him. Jessie and Mary also took bus trips to Gallipolis, and I traveled by bus on one trip and hitchhiked from Bowling Green during two school vacations to spend them with Joe. I found conditions in the hospital depressing; it appeared to me that the objective of the staff was to separate epileptics from society, waiting for them to die at an early age. The male patients lived in an open barrack, which was under-standable for military personnel but hardly appropriate for epileptics who needed privacy, especially after a grand mal seizure. Joe contracted tubercu-losis at Gallipolis and was transferred to the state tuberculosis hospital at Mount Vernon. He died there on January 7, 1950, at age twenty-eight, and was buried in Calvary Cemetery in Lorain.

Grandmother had observed daily the pain and suffering of two of her grandchildren. She had lived in abject poverty most of her life in a country in which she was an alien. We never heard her complain of any physical ailment or of her status in life. We believed she was indestructible, a tower of strength and indomitable will in a tiny body the size of a preadolescent girl. She was a great lady in every respect, and she instilled in us a moral order that she was not able to define in any structured form. Her unwritten credo was to always be good and do right by everyone you meet. She emphasized strict observance of the law.

When I was fourteen years old, she sent me on an errand. I ambled along Vine Avenue, chatting with buddies and stopping to watch acquaintances roll dice for pennies on the elementary school lawn (after school hours). I became so absorbed in the gambling that I ignored the passage of time and joined in the game. Suddenly I felt a sharp sting on my rump and turned to see Mama with a stern look on her face and a switch in her hand. She did not say a word. The group broke up, the boys muttering as they shuffled away, while I stood there motionless, facing my grandmother. I turned and resumed my assigned task.

Mama raised us as practicing Catholics, requiring attendance at Sunday mass, confession, and communion. There were Mexican implementations of Catholic beliefs; we demonstrated a deep reverence for Saint Mary, the patron saint of Mexico, by observing the annual novena to Our Lady of Guadalupe and attending nine consecutive nights of rosary and benediction services at Saint John Catholic Church.

Although Mama rarely expressed her emotional pain, it could be glimpsed on occasion. It was heartrending to watch her face fall with unshed tears when the postman passed without leaving mail after not having heard from Joe for several weeks. By the late 1940s her health had begun to deteriorate and she was hospitalized for various ailments. She had not been informed of Joe's critical condition, and she died on December 26, 1950, of kidney failure without knowing of his death. She is buried in a gravesite adjoining Joe's burial plot, with a common headstone. We estimated her age to be seventy-three years at the time of her death.

✿ ✿ ✿

CHAPTER EIGHT

Panama and the Canal Zone

I started to work for the Firestone Tire and Rubber Company of Akron, Ohio, in April 1951. As a physical science assistant in the Research Division, I conducted laboratory and field tests and gathered scientific data on prototype models of military weapons. The division was under contract to develop a 106mm (4.2 inches) recoilless rifle and ammunition for the Pentagon's U.S. Army Research and Development Office. The objective was to provide infantry units with an antitank weapon for direct fire missions that were not feasible with 105mm howitzers.

My first assignment was to conduct firing tests of prototype models at the Erie Proving Ground near Port Clinton, Ohio, and collect the data for scientists designing various versions of the rifle and its ammunition. We fired inert slugs from the firing line toward a restricted area of the Lake Erie shore and studied the internal ballistics of the weapon. We also employed a crude test stand with chamber and gun tube fabricated to match the technical characteristics of a recoilless rifle from which we fired various inert projectile types at a twelve-foot-square plywood target one thousand yards downrange; the points of impact were recorded for evaluation by scientists and engineers to determine the exterior ballistics performance of the projectile design.

A year later I was transferred to the Firestone main plant in Akron to assist scientists and engineers in the design of weapon and ammunition and to conduct laboratory tests prior to testing models on the firing line. One of my major duties over the next two years was to coordinate projectile designs with engineers at the Picatinny Arsenal in New Jersey and to fill test rounds with high explosive. I then sent these to the Aberdeen Proving Ground in

Maryland and arranged for the rounds to be fired while I gathered pertinent data. At the Frankford Arsenal in Philadelphia I discussed the status of our work with government scientists and engineers who were competitively developing a different version of the weapon.

Working with engineers on various projects convinced me to try engineering as a more satisfying career. After three years in the Research Division, I transferred to the Tire Development Department and enrolled at the University of Akron for night and weekend classes in mechanical engineering. Three years later I passed both national Professional Engineer examinations (sixteen hours written and two hours oral) in Columbus, Ohio, and was licensed by the state of Ohio to practice as a professional engineer.

Leticia Carles Guardia graduated from Bowling Green State University in June 1951. We agreed to a period of time apart to test the strength of our feelings for each other. She returned to her hometown in Panama and accepted a teaching position. A year later we established a wedding date and were married in Panama on October 11, 1952. After the honeymoon, we returned to Akron and started a family. Joseph was our first child. Our daughter, Jo, followed almost exactly a year later.

I found the work at Firestone satisfying, both financially and professionally. Ten years earlier, following a three-week trip to Mexico, I'd wondered if life in a Spanish-speaking country could help me resolve the infrequent moments of racial alienation I still retained from my childhood. Lety and I decided that we needed to directly address the resolution of that problem. As a first step toward that goal, I submitted an application for a mechanical engineer vacancy in the Panama Canal Zone.

If selected for the position, the move would allow for a smooth transition between life in an American community in the Canal Zone and the Spanish-speaking environment of Lety's hometown 150 kilometers away in the Panama interior (a demographic term for the inner region of the country, west of Panama City).

In February 1957 I accepted an offer from the U.S. Navy for a job as a mechanical engineer at Fort Amador in the Canal Zone. Four months after selling our house in Akron and moving our family and belongings to the Canal Zone, the Navy's engineering office was consolidated into the Puerto Rico office as a cost-saving measure. Not wanting to transfer to Puerto Rico, I sought to fill an engineering vacancy in the U.S. Army Caribbean Command, also located at Fort Amador. By coincidence, the officer who interviewed me had served as commanding officer of the Erie Proving Ground at the time that

Firestone operated the classified field-test site. He was familiar with the work we had done there and he selected me for the position in which I would advise him on weapons acquisition, operation, and maintenance.

My work in the army's ordnance section was the turning point of my career. Three men were directly responsible for preparing me to serve the subsequent thirty years of my professionally rewarding association with the U.S. Army. Colonel Elmer Grubbs and his executive officer, Lieutenant Colonel Ralph Wells, were a positive influence with their principled beliefs in dedicated service to the army and our country. They encouraged me to apply for an army reserve commission, for which I qualified with my academic degrees, civilian engineer experience, and prior service in the U.S. Marine Corps.

I had turned down an opportunity for a reserve commission in the Marine Corps by failing to attend the second voluntary phase of a summer tour of active duty in the Platoon Leaders Class (PLC). It was conducted each summer at Quantico, Virginia (the PLC is the Marine Corps' version of the Army's Reserve Officers Training Corps). My second summer tour conflicted with the summer session I needed to take to complete my degree at BGSU. I had to drop out of the PLC program—no excused absences allowed. In 1958, after appearing before a board of army officers, I was commissioned in the army reserve by direct appointment.

Col. John C. Nickerson replaced Colonel Grubbs after the latter completed his overseas tour. Jack Nickerson was one of the most honorable and dedicated officers it has been my pleasure to know and serve. An unfortunate experience at the Redstone Arsenal in Alabama resulted in his being relieved after unauthorized missile information was leaked to a Washington columnist by someone under his command. He was transferred to the Canal Zone, where he became my immediate supervisor. He was a brilliant officer who could have moved higher in rank had he not made a mistake which he sincerely believed was the right thing to do for the army and the nation. He was caught up in a major behind-the-scenes battle between high-level officers of the army and air force. The controversy was over roles and missions under study by the Department of Defense concerning the development and operation of guided missiles.

We worked on plans to install army defensive missile systems in the Canal Zone to deter enemy aircraft from targeting Panama Canal facilities. The international situation at that time involved concerns by the United States that the close relations developing between Fidel Castro and the Union of Soviet Socialist Republics could lead to the possibility of guided missiles

Col. Frank S. Mendez, U.S. Army Reserve, October 1973. *U.S. Army photograph.*

being launched from Cuba to vulnerable American facilities like those in the Panama Canal.

Colonel Nickerson named me as his project engineer with a mission to establish sites for deployment of the first battalion of HAWK missile systems to be sent overseas. We conducted studies on the coverage of incoming aircraft by acquisition and range radars, the optimum positions of battery control centers and missile launchers, and the potential of nearby hills to radar-mask low-level flights of incoming aircraft. We also established maintenance capabilities to repair missile system components on-site and in our ordnance maintenance shops. The HAWK sites were constructed, HAWK battalion personnel arrived, and within thirty days the first HAWK missile batteries overseas became operational.

Lety and I considered Carol and Jack Nickerson to be two of our closest friends. After completing his overseas tour, he was assigned to the White Sands Missile Range in New Mexico. Carol and Jack died in an automobile accident on March 2, 1964, near Alamogordo, New Mexico.

As I continued my civilian career with the army in more responsible positions, my army reserve career continued apace. I was promoted to colonel after earning diplomas from the U.S. Army Command and General Staff College in Fort Leavenworth, Kansas, and the U.S. Army War College at Carlisle Barracks in Pennsylvania. As a mobilization designee, I served six tours of active duty in the Pentagon.

My most important assignment was as commander of an organized reserve unit, the Balboa Detachment of the National Wartime Information Security Organization (NWISO), which consisted of a headquarters in the New York area and twenty-one detachments covering important mail, ship, cablegram, and aircraft points-of-entry into the United States.

Each unit consisted of fourteen officers and one enlisted person; on declaration of war, we were to hire three-to-four hundred civilians to gather intelligence data for distribution to appropriate wartime security organizations. The NWISO detachments assembled each year for a two-week tour of active duty training, our operational exercises were conducted at a military base in the United States. The entire concept was based on World War II strategy; it was outmoded by the mid-1970s, and NWISO was abolished by the Department of Defense.

I retired from the U.S. Army Reserve in October 1980 and was awarded the Legion of Merit by Headquarters, Department of the Army, Washington, D.C.

※

My civilian career progressed in the U.S. Army Tropic Test Center as technical adviser, chief of the Materiel Test Division, and technical director. We conducted research and tests on the ability of soldiers and their equipment to function in a tropic environment. Test reports on the capability of their equipment to meet specifications when used in a tropic environment were forwarded to army research and development laboratories.

As I rose higher in grade, the governor of the Canal Zone asked my supervisor, the commander of the U.S. Army Tropic Test Center, to permit me to take on an unpaid public service as an added duty. I was sworn in as a member of the five-person Canal Zone Board of Registration for Architects and Professional Engineers, on which I served two successive five-year terms, including one year as chairman. The board was responsible for enforcement of Title 35, Code of Federal Regulations (Canal Zone Regulations) pertaining to the practice of architecture and engineering. We ensured that applicants for a professional engineer or architect license had the requisite academic and experience levels; we also administered semiannual tests that were being taken throughout the United States on the same two days. Board members were required to attend an annual one-week conference of the National Council of Engineering Examiners, a body that sought to establish and maintain a consistent set of standards for the practice of engineering among the fifty states, the Canal Zone, and Puerto Rico. The governor honored me with the Panama Canal Honorary Public Service Award for my service.

I was also asked by the governor, in his other role as president of the Panama Canal Company, to serve as a member of the board of trustees and as executive vice president of the non-profit Canal Zone United Way Corporation. I chaired the monthly board meetings for him, approving plans for annual drives, presentation of a $6 million budget, allocation of resources, and the review and recording of final results.

Except in official dealings at work, I spoke Spanish with most Panamanian employees and in all commercial and industrial enterprises. Although we resided in the Canal Zone throughout my career, we lived like a middle-class Panamanian family, speaking English and Spanish at home, and Spanish only with relatives and Panamanian friends.

※

The Canal Zone was established in 1903 by treaty between the United States and the Republic of Panama. Its borders ran five miles on each side of the fifty-mile-long Panama Canal. The boundaries of Panama City on the Pacific side of the isthmus and of Colon on the Atlantic side were not changed; the final design of the canal centerline was, and is, a few hundred yards from each city.

By 1957 when my family and I arrived and took up residence, the Canal Zone could be compared to a huge military reservation in a five-hundred-square-mile Florida county. It had a civil government; a federal district courthouse; two municipal judgeships; churches of various faiths; a police department; fire stations; commissaries; movie theaters; athletic fields and mini-stadiums; hospitals; American Legion, Jewish War Brethren, and Veterans of Foreign Wars clubhouses; a yacht club; a Masonic lodge; an Elks club; schools up to and including a junior college (a Florida State University branch granted bachelor's degrees a few years later); and "racially segregated" civilian housing, legally referred to as "Local Nationals Communities," populated over 90 percent by black Panamanian citizens. They were Panama Canal Company "key employees," proud descendants of West Indian immigrants who had helped build the Panama Canal (the other civilian residents were Panamanian Latinos, also considered key employees).

Life in the Canal Zone for an American citizen was an experience unmatched by any lifestyle in any state in the United States. In order to reside in the Canal Zone, one had to be employed by a U.S. government agency—the unemployment rate was 0 percent. It was a form of benign socialism from cradle to grave. Employees drew wages from the government, resided in government quarters, and had children delivered by government employed doctors and nurses in a federal hospital; their children were taught by federally employed teachers in government schools, and when an employee or family member died, they were buried in a federal cemetery.

The major government organizations were the Canal Zone government; the Panama Canal Company; and the U.S. Army, U.S. Air Force, U.S. Navy, and U. S. Marine Corps. The Panama Canal Company and the military services provided housing for their employees in small towns and on military reservations. We lived in the Curundu housing area of Fort Clayton, the largest military base, associating at all age levels with military and civilian family members. Three of our children, Terry, Michael, and Carol were born in the Canal Zone (Carol is named after our late friend, Carol Nickerson). Our five children developed close friendships with children of military officers, enlisted persons, and other civilians as they advanced from kindergarten to high school graduation. Since military families were in the Canal Zone for a three-year tour, their departures left several of our children with a sadness that took a while to overcome. Like "military brats," however, they learned to prepare themselves for a forthcoming severance by gradually adjusting the bonds of friendship as the departure date approached.

We mixed with two other family groups—Panama Canal civilian employees and Panamanians who did not live in the Canal Zone. We were fortunate to enjoy the close association with such a wide range of family backgrounds as we lengthened our stay in Panama.

Americans living in the Canal Zone were informally referred to as "zonians," a derisive term when used by Panamanians but not acknowledged as such by zonians. Panamanians defined a zonian as one who lived like a colonial, isolated in the Canal Zone, enjoying a "foreign" culture in the heart of a sovereign nation. Our family was an exception to both views. We adapted readily to the use of Spanish in our everyday dealings with Panamanians and lived among them, for weeks at a time, in the hills 150 kilometers from Fort Clayton. During our thirty-year stay there we did not feel like foreigners in their country, and people in the interior did not outwardly consider us as such. In no way was the love and attachment to our country diminished by our friendship with the people of Panama.

My job as a U.S. Army civilian was not much different from the duties of my counterparts at army proving grounds in the United States. I spoke frequently with them by telephone and often met with them in Panama or on their home base on official visits. The U.S. Army Tropic Test Center was one of eight subordinate units of the U.S. Army Test and Evaluation Command. As such, we conducted our activities very much in line with the organizational structure at places as diverse as the Yuma Proving Ground in Arizona, Fort Greely in Alaska, and the Aberdeen Proving Ground in Maryland. At least four or five times a year, I had to make official visits to proving grounds, the Pentagon, and academic institutions for studies and training in management and technical subjects. It was a personally rewarding experience that I enjoyed immensely. I often marveled at the fact that someone born of Mexican migrant farm workers in the United States could be presented with such great opportunities to advance himself and his family to a socioeconomic status so different from that of his forebears.

The Canal Zone was essentially an American enclave in the heart of Panama. Many Panama Canal Company employees were proud descendants of American expatriates who had built, operated, and maintained the canal. Over the years their patriotism had grown so strong that newly arrived Americans could be excused for thinking that it seemed to be somewhat chauvinistic in manner. A case in point was the origins of the January 1964 riots in which four American soldiers and twenty Panamanians died.

There are differing views on this subject. In my view, the riots could have been avoided but for an orderly but questionably proper demonstration by American students at Balboa High School in the Canal Zone. After years of increasingly uneasy foreign relations between the Republic of Panama and the United States over sovereignty of the Canal Zone, President John F. Kennedy issued an executive order in 1963 for the Panama flag to fly alongside the United States flag at five selected locations in the Canal Zone, one of them being Balboa High School. Previously, the Panama flag had never been raised officially in the Canal Zone; in earlier years there had been symbolic "invasions" of the Canal Zone by Panamanians (mostly students) legally entering the Canal Zone, planting small Panamanian flags in the ground, and rushing back to Panama City a few blocks away. Reaction by Americans was mainly humorous—no attempt was made to stop them or initiate pursuit. Canal Zone police gathered the flags with care, announced that no law had been broken, and invited the owners to claim the flags. They were not claimed.

After a flagpole for the Panama flag was erected at Balboa High School, unauthorized American students raised the American flag on the old pole and indirectly blocked access to the new pole a few feet away. They conducted all-night vigils to prevent anyone from lowering the American flag, which was nominally performed on school days at 5:00 P.M. Their parents and other "patriots" encouraged them to continue the demonstration, bringing them food and soft drinks and "standing watch" over them. Canal Zone police effectively encouraged them by a "kids will be kids" attitude, watching complacently from patrol cars parked in front of the building. If the American Embassy in Panama or the U.S. State Department objected, citing a negative impact of the incident on relations with the Republic of Panama, it was not evident to American residents in the area.

I drove past the high school with my family on the afternoon of January 9, 1964, and paused to chat with acquaintances among the police. I wondered out loud how Canal Zone authorities, who were federal employees, could allow this violation of a presidential edict without attempting to enforce it.

What happened after that is history. That same afternoon, a group of Panamanian high school students, accompanied by some of their teachers from Panama's *Instituto Nacional,* marched to Balboa High School, carrying an old, historic Panama flag, and made a courteous request to have it raised on the empty flagpole. There are differing versions about what happened next. At any rate, the Panama flag was torn during the packed emotional grouping around the flagpoles. Panamanians claimed that Americans deliberately tore their flag and forced them out of the Canal Zone. American officials claimed the flag was torn because of its age-weakened condition and rough handling by its excited supporters—police reported that nobody chased the Panamanians out of the Canal Zone; they rushed back to Panama City of their own accord, turning over trash barrels, throwing rocks at residential quarters, and shouting that they were being chased by Americans who had prevented them from raising their flag and torn it. For the next few days there was shooting, looting, and the setting of fires by Panamanian elements along the borders on both sides of the isthmus.

Order was restored by the U.S. Southern Command and the *Guardia Nacional* (Panama police force), the latter taking several days to respond while people were dying in the streets.

The January 1964 disturbances contributed to the creation of a patriotic fervor among Panamanians to eliminate the Canal Zone infrastructure from their territory. They were tired of what they viewed as a paternalistic attitude by the United States in the implementation of the 1903 treaty. In the minds of many well-educated, responsible Panamanian leaders of academic, civic, commercial, and professional fields (many of whom had attended universities from California to New York and considered themselves friends of the United States), it was time for their American friends to let them grow up and manage their own affairs of state. The United States Senate agreed, and in 1977 passed the new Panama Canal Treaty that eliminated the Canal Zone in 1979 and transferred ownership and operation of the Panama Canal to the Republic of Panama in December 1999.

As noted earlier, relations between Panama and the United States had deteriorated after the 1964 riots as Panama continued to assert its prerogatives on the interpretation of the 1903 treaty and a 1955 amendment. Both sides gradually developed a spirit of cooperation leading to an agreement to negotiate a new treaty for control and, ultimately, ownership of the Panama Canal. The discussions ended abruptly when a military junta deposed the democratically elected president of Panama and his cabinet on October 11, 1968.

For the next twenty-one years, a military dictatorship ruled the country, establishing pseudo-democratic governments with fraudulent elections that placed handpicked puppets in executive, legislative, and judicial positions. The military dictator, in civilian clothes, and as "head of state," signed the new Panama Canal Treaty, which was to relinquish to Panama on December 31, 1999, ownership of the canal and its industrial, commercial, residential, and educational facilities, and military bases, all of it valued at $30 billion.

As the end of the century approached, the U.S. Southern Command reduced its presence; it closed the bases of Fort Amador, Fort Sherman, Quarry Heights, Fort Clayton, the Corozal industrial area, Rodman Naval Station, Albrook Air Force Station, and finally the Howard Air Force Base, which locked its gates on October 24, 1999.

While in Panama on a short visit, I toured the base on the last day of its existence as an American military facility. It was closed to visitors, but the air police squad on duty for the final twenty-four hours, after checking my retired military identification, allowed me to enter for a last look at the installation that my family and I had used for over thirty years. It was uninhabited; the housing areas, flight line, barracks, training and field exercise locations, administrative and logistics buildings, elementary school, roads, and grounds appeared to be immaculately maintained, months after the last active unit departed. Each time I stepped from the car, I was surrounded by families of coatimundis (feral raccoon-like creatures) looking for scraps of food formerly stolen from overturned garbage cans or begged from residents who violated base regulations by feeding them. The next morning I watched the televised formal ceremony in which United States officials "turned over the keys" to representatives of the government of Panama. The coatimundi families were very much in evidence, milling around the new owners as if to establish their claim as residents transferred with the property.

American military families viewed their three years in Panama as just another tour in a foreign country, respecting the laws of their "hosts" and trying to maintain good relations with the host country. My family and I were of the same mind. We had come to Panama to be part of a Spanish-speaking culture where I could determine in what direction my future lay. To make that determination I needed to experience the life of someone who did not stand out as a "foreigner." We spent much time in the Panama interior (where English was not spoken or understood), mixing with relatives and close friends, away from the overpowering influence of the Canal Zone.

Those early years of my stay in Panama were instrumental in clarifying my unwarranted sensitivity to incidents or words addressing race. An atmosphere in which I was so totally accepted by a community helped me erase the alienation I had felt in Ohio. The U.S. Army also influenced my transition from a person searching for an identity to one who would never have to question this for the rest of his life. In the 1950s the Army was in the forefront of American organizations aggressively pursuing the elimination of racially divisive attitudes and practices among its members. My close daily association with military personnel and their families at all ranks gradually gave me the wisdom to bury the alienation that had haunted me so much of my life. It was gone by the early 1960s.

On retirement from the federal service, I was awarded the Oak Leaf Cluster to the Meritorious Civilian Service Medal. I did not earn the medals entirely on my own. Lety contributed immensely—her energy and outstanding organizational ability in creating a beautiful family atmosphere allowed me the flexibility to concentrate my attention on the demanding requirements of my job.

Our five children graduated from Balboa High School and went on to college and life in the United States. They have never expressed doubt about their identity as Americans, or had reason to think that others would question it. The three generations of our family are completely at home in the United States, with a quiet pride in being Americans and a deep respect for our Latino heritage.